£2.50

GW01418055

AUTUMN DAWN

AUTUMN DAWN

Triumph over Eating Disorders

Ann Cox

The Book Guild Ltd
Sussex, England

The Book Guild Ltd.
25 High Street,
Lewes, Sussex

First published 1995
© Ann Cox 1995
Set in Times
Typesetting by Poole Typesetting (Wessex) Ltd.
Bournemouth, Dorset.
Printed in Great Britain by
Bookcraft (Bath) Ltd.

A catalogue record for this book is
available from the British Library

ISBN 1 85776 010 7

CON`ENTS

ACKNOWLEDGEMENTS

I had very much hoped that one year after leaving hospital, I would be able to write this book, but I discovered twelve months to be a very short period in the sometimes painstaking process of discovering about 'normality'. Full recovery takes much longer, hence it is now well over five years since I walked free of anorexia and bulimia nervosa.

Occasionally, in the early part, survival meant taking each day as it came. I don't think there was ever a single thing that kept me going; day-to-day routines, my help-line, initiating two self-help groups, deciding to get married and my ambition to put my experiences to good use have all been pegs to hang on to. Each were events on the horizon, just as was learning to walk again (in the true sense of the word), and coping with being disabled as a result of my eating disorder, which also meant me being forced into early retirement – another great adjustment. Only now, so many months later, am I able to really start to look ahead. Anorexia and bulimia nervosa are behind me, and I'm determined not to live in the shadow of my medical history.

I will not accept the label 'ex-anorectic' either, nor the suggestion that once suffered an eating disorder, always an eating disorder. There are certainly days when I'm emotionally shaky, probably just like everyone else, but equally there are fantastic days full only of laughter, and these well outweigh the others. The shaky days are either due to PMT or just sudden whims of lack of confidence as self-doubt rears its head. And I suppose that's a normal trait – self-doubt versus self-esteem. So, I go on holding hands, laughing and hanging on to everything good. I take life 'by the horns', thanking God for my friends, and also thanking Him for me being able to be a friend to others – a special bonus, that one. I really 'go for it' – giving, receiving and sharing are marvellous gifts; I knew nothing of these for thirty eight years, nor did I know about love – a hugely intimidating thing at first. But I do now, and for that and for being free to express my emotions, I have to acknowledge the help of so many people.

During the rather arduous journey into the prison of anorexia and then out of it onto the road to recovery, I have met many special people. I cannot acknowledge you all; some of your names I'm afraid I don't recall, so I shall list a few, and would ask those of you not named to be assured that your presence in my journey most certainly had its place.

Into the limelight must go Aurélie Rubié, Dr Stephen Kidman, The Reverend Paul Renyard and friends in Bournemouth and my dearest friend Pam Hedges, and her husband Ron – with whom, on my road to recovery, I learned to laugh and cry, whilst I spent several recuperating months in their home. Most important of all, is my best friend and husband, Stephen, whose continued love and support during the comparatively short life we have shared together, and whilst writing *Autumn Dawn* (which certainly produced some tears and heart-ache) makes me the proudest wife in the world.

My thanks also to Eileen Remedious, Julia Buss, Sandra Porter, Irene Bucknall, Tim Boone, Mark Parker, Trevor Freeman, Pamela (Pammy) Nickels, Esmé Wheeler, Gill Coleman, Janet and Roger Bourne, Jo and Gail Bourne, Frank and Gladys Mann, Sue Gilks, Sheena Danson, Douglas Read, Brenda Maclean, Stuart and June Clarke, Becky Owen, Becci Hayward, Ann Callaghan, Kirsty Paddon, Sue French, Jan Hinds, Claire Richards, Louise Miller, Phillipa Keast, Bess and Frank Marsh, Elsie King, Monica Jones, Muff Cotton, Liz Whiting, Muriel and Cyril

Lawton, Janice Seare, Betty Kendall, Doreen Wilks, Sheila Perring, Val Wood, Val Renyard, Sue Davies (from Threshold), Chris Tredgold, Peter Bermingham, Neil Joughin and his team, Jane Cockerton, Clare Dyas and, finally, Dr D J Cameron.

To you all, thank you.

To my dear friends Pam and Ron Hedges, for their continued love and encouragement, and to Stephen, my best friend and husband, forever there to hold hands and exchange hugs.

Written for all those who have suffered or are suffering an eating disorder, be they a friend, relative or the people themselves, and for all those yet to be confronted with such trauma.

INTRODUCTION

Do you or does anyone, I wonder, know the real beauty of watching the early dawn in autumn, watching the deep orange ball of the sun as it rises, going on to add some warmth to the day; the real joy, too, of discovering how amazing and qualitative life can be, or what it's really like to discover Living and Fun – and fresh air, and peanut-butter sandwiches with watercress? As well as the joys of being able to see, smell, and walk through fields of bluebells, daffodils, hyacinths and poppies, singing your heart out as you go! I discovered this at the rather advanced age of thirty eight and three quarters; being born was purely an event, and I'm afraid I remember little of those formative years.

This book, my story, is for all you who know only that blackness and hate the daylight as I did, and it is also for those of you, whether you be a sufferer or otherwise. It is an attempt to describe the agonies of the prison sentence of an eating disorder, seemingly served in solitary confinement, with no apparent set date for freedom, but also the POSITIVE truth that there *is* a way out. There is hope – and that doesn't come through death. I'm alive, well, fully recovered and I'm no longer crying out, 'Help me' or 'God, please let me die'. *Autumn Dawn* is my experience, and in the words of a hymn to which I was introduced, I 'pass it on', hoping it will help others.

As a sufferer of an eating disorder for twenty eight years, I existed in a hell on earth, which became a vicious circle of self-hate, and hating everything that represents life, ie, pleasure, fun, change and even breathing. There was no room for laughter, only denial and deprivation in a most abusive and self-destructive way. So abusive and destructive in fact, that towards the end I felt I was a victim of something totally alien. The devil perhaps.

Only in looking back, can I say how much I suffered, suffered not only physically, mentally and emotionally, but also spiritually in that total solitariness, isolation and abandonment, which, however close one's friends and relatives are, or may be, becomes a terrifying experience for the lonely being. I'm no longer lonely now, though; I fought against, and won my long battle with anorexia/bulimia nervosa together with the other intrinsic symptoms this rather unfortunately stereotype labelled disorder encompasses, something which few people appreciate, because, as with any of the eating disorders, it manifests itself solely in a twenty four-hour obsession with food, weight, body, shape and size. A seemingly totally weird, peculiar and incomprehensible thing, but which in reality, is a symptom signifying something requiring far more in-depth and serious consideration, attention and, most important of all perhaps, UNDERSTANDING – by both sufferers and non-sufferers alike. I thus feel my years of problems centring around food, and the desire/need to have some control in my life, can only be put to good use. And should be. And perhaps I can help to justify the need for that serious attention and understanding.

I feel honesty to be the essence in *Autumn Dawn*, and so must admit that I still bear some scars from my years of anorexia and bulimia nervosa, which I describe as a psychophysical illness or disorder. I am registered physically disabled now, experiencing considerable mobility difficulties and constant pain, as a consequence of the severity of my sheer self-abuse, and the chronicity of it. There are also a few emotional scars – allowing myself indulgences, for example, and accepting as real that thing called 'unconditional love', but it is not these alone that I speak of though, because there is much about which to be positive. I am finally free – to live, love, laugh, be happy, sad, angry, pleased, or whatever, as appropriate, and feel OK, because at last I have found self-confidence and self-respect, although occasionally self-doubt wins over self-respect, and I fall back into the non-deserving patterns of thought, the need to deprive myself, because of guilt and anger, and the wish, therefore, to 'have nothing'. Perhaps this is, to some extent anyway, normal; in fact I'm constantly assured by many people who know me that feelings of unworthiness are something most people experience, and anyway such thought patterns of mine do eventually go away, without me acting on them in an unconstructive way. Rather the opposite – I go ahead and enjoy that self-indulgence! And I give or exchange hugs with Stephen for the sheer pleasure of it. No other reason! So I believe, even more assuredly, that I do have a very encouraging and important story to tell.

As each day passes I continue the process of throwing away my crutches with an almost bloody-minded impudence, relying on grit, gumption, belief in myself, and the grace and goodness of my dear friends, parents-in-law, and Stephen, my friend, my love, my husband. The crutches of which I speak are not those I use to walk – they are different, they are good fun, enabling me to mobilise (and sometimes poke people with!) – but rather the emotional ones. All this, I hope, will help you to realise and believe that although I, and many others, have been, or are being tossed about by life, *my* feet have at last firmly touched terra firma, and if no-one else does (but I assure you they do!), I congratulate myself on having re-joined the human race; on having put back the Ooohs and Aaahs, and wonderment into such simple aspects of mortal life, such as laughing, and even crying when I see the beauty of the face of a pansy peeping through the undergrowth. I'm no longer talking of An(n) Orexia now, this is Ann Mann, née Ann Cox:

> *I'm not just a face in a crowd,*
> *Or a number in a file.*
> *I'm not a brick in a wall,*
> *Or just a cog in a wheel.*

xiii

I'm not a log in a pile,
Nor just a fish in the sea.
– I'm far more special than that,
– I'm ME.

(Taken from an entry in my diary in November 1990).

And every me in the world is special even with your vulner-
abilities and weaknesses, so please read on. You might just
discover why.

IN THE BEGINNING?

I feel such comfort and pleasure at 4 stones, even though sometimes I feel fat, it is so reassuring to curl up, with my elbow resting in the hollow of my pelvis, to feel the sharpness of my hip bones and to be able to count every rib, see each vertebra, and the hollow at the base of my sternum. Seeing every bone stick out and the rest of me sunken in is my raison d'être.
(1982 diary, dated August 1st)

– My weight had risen to four stones three pounds. –

When I was eighteen I began what seemed to be an all-out pursuit of thinness. Nothing else, nobody nor anything mattered, everyone was at the mercy of my obsession with food, weight, shape and size. My kneecaps and thighs had to be the same size, likewise my wrists and the tops of my arms. Every bone, everywhere, had to be visible – if they weren't, then I took more than my daily 'fix' of 200 laxatives, 30 diuretics and 6 suppositories. This served several purposes: one, a punishment, for not being thin enough; two, something that would cause me further pain, (physical pain), and three, an obscure way of relieving myself of the mental torment I was going through, ie, stopping feeling anything emotionally.

I never won that pursuit of thinness. I was never thin enough, despite losing a drastic five stones in six months. I'd almost stopped eating and drinking completely and weighed in at under four stones (I am five feet five and a half inches). All I gained from this really, was a label – I was an anorectic, I had anorexia nervosa (which in later years was to

1

encompass bulimia nervosa), but I thought I had gained something else – control. I loved the feeling of being empty, even though it was painful and I was hungry. I thrived on depriving myself, and the more empty I felt, the better. The more I deprived and denied myself anything to fill it, the better. Although I did not realise it, I was dancing with death and my dance was becoming a *danse macabre*. Furthermore, no-one else realised it either, or if they did they did not tell me. To me it meant nothing, it was too late – I was experiencing a peculiar and wonderful buzz and sense of euphoria from the weight loss and no food, and I seemed to have loads of (nervous) energy despite this severe self-abuse and deprivation. It was a euphoria so great it kept me going for the next twelve years.

Eighteen years old also earmarked something else though, but something which no-one else could see and hence couldn't understand. I really hated myself and was weighted down by heavy emotions, including shame, guilt, and anger, all repressed throughout my childhood. There was such a dreadful tiredness, too (even though I speak of having so much energy at the same time), a tiredness which was far more than just that. It was a mental, physical and spiritual exhaustion, emanating from despair, and from what, only two years ago now, I recognise to be fear and sadness; two emotions that had become grafted onto the others and which, at first, were hard to acknowledge and accept, let alone recognise.

By losing all that weight, I had also started to live on borrowed time. Regarding my self-esteem, my sell-by date had long gone – I'd gone off, I stank, I felt like shit! I was fit only for the gutter and boy, was I going to do anything and everything to lower myself into it. In other words, eighteen years old was too late a stage at which to recognise I was ill. My emotional disorder, at least the seeds, had started long ago. Now, of course, sure people knew something was wrong, but only because of my physical appearance. They did not appreciate my dis-ease (ie, my uneasiness with myself and with life). The symptoms they saw were easily solved –

eat! It seemed that everyone thought the 'problem' just centred around poor eating; therefore the answer was easy – eat properly. Inevitably the pressures came to eat, and I think it was at this point that I began to be angry – with everybody, as well as with myself. I felt devastated – no-one could help. Even as a child no-one helped. No-one, least of all me, understood, and I suppose upon reflection I realise I needed to ask for more than help. I needed help to help and understand myself. As it was there was nobody there:

When I tried talking to you,
You only seemed to hear, not listen.
When I made mistakes,
You found my weaknesses funny.
Even when I told you my dreams,
You laughed.
You never seemed to understand.
So I stopped trying to communicate – and ate
*   instead.*
Then you were amused because I was enjoying
*   my food,*
You seemed insensitive to everything I needed
*   emotionally.*
You cared for my physical and educational needs
*   to perfection*
But the me inside became impoverished.
– so I went into myself,
And became imprisoned.
But I will get out,
I'll eat a banquet one day,
And what's more, I went in as a child,
But I'll emerge released and free to be recognised
*   as me,*
As a woman

(Written 18th May 1990, during my final hospital admission – addressed to my parents.)

The title for this chapter has a question mark after it because I strongly feel that when my weight loss was apparent, and people saw that I was unwell, it was much later than when the seeds were first planted, much later than when the problems were developing. The real beginning goes much further back, but as I wanted to capture your attention, whether you be reading this book out of curiosity, as a sufferer, a family relative of someone who is ill, or just simply as someone flicking through it on a library shelf or in a bookshop, I've tried to paint a brief and rapid picture of the devastation of my anorexia/bulimia nervosa – something with which perhaps many of you can identify, and would therefore perhaps like to read on. So many people, male (twenty two per cent of the callers on my help-line are male) and female, are suffering an eating disorder and want to 'get better' but 'can't'. Actually, they can! But I firmly believe that unless one CHOOSES to recover, life can only improve, rather than become really qualitative; it merely becomes an extension to an existence, with many limitations. Fighting to make a full recovery is worth it. Winning my own battle has proved such a triumph, in more ways than one, the main one being that I'm alive, well and happy.

ELEVEN YEARS OLD
– BEFORE AND AFTER

I feel it important to say right now that my recollections of events and times during my illness are at times hazy. I guess my memory became impaired and I developed a safety mechanism by forgetting, thus pushing down all the deep hurts. I have decided to start at eleven years old because there was a big event in my life then – I passed the eleven plus (after much worrying and many tears), and was able to turn right at the bottom of the front garden gate to go to the grammar school, instead of left to the secondary school. However, some events before and afterwards are quite possibly not in chronological order, although I'm not sure it really matters. I was a child and unhappy.

I was born in Tunbridge Wells, on 30th January 1952, the only child of a Welsh mother and a Londoner father. Soon after my arrival (my parents were in their thirties), my father secured a good job in London as a quantity surveyor/architect, and we accordingly moved house, nearer to London, to St Albans, Hertfordshire, where to outsiders, anyway, we lived a very comfortable and quite well-to-do life, at 24 New Greens Avenue. I was given music, ballet and horseriding lessons, as well as elocution training, and perhaps even then some resentment began to manifest itself. Life was centring round achievements, exams, certificates and speaking 'properly'. They were all going to be 'strings to my bow', but blow the bow, what was wrong with ME just as I was? I can understand the pleasure my family might have derived from being able to afford to give me these 'added extras', which, of course they had never had, and perhaps, too, their pride when I passed my exams (which I always did, but which always left room for improvement) – they had a successful daughter. The importance of that however may have been in continuing the line of doctorates on my mother's side, and/or being considered to be of high intelligence, gifted and clever, or talented even. But was it really for my own well-being, or something for outsiders to see? Was it, too, something on which my parents could thrive?

At a very early age, it was quite apparent to me that my parents were experiencing marital difficulties, and I felt to blame. They argued over me, they separated – albeit temporarily – because of me, and they never divorced, because of me. I couldn't win! They had to be what my mother called 'responsible parents'; a child needed a mother and a father. She was right. I was a child, and I needed a mother and a father, but ones that I could call Mummy and Daddy, and who would let me have a party dress, watch television, lick an ice cream walking along the road, one that I had perhaps bought with some pocket money, and maybe even let me 'do nothing'. Be idle! Quite probably my parents feel they really did do their best. I'll never know – we've lost each other. However, I'm sure they did what they thought was right at the time. Although I feel no bitterness and do not want to betray them entirely, I would like them to know I now have a party dress, I enjoy watching television when Steve and I choose to, I've had quite a few ice creams and I intend to lick many more, and yep! I sometimes do nothing, hard though I sometimes find it. 'Tis fun to be idle occasionally!

More relevant to the nature of my story, I recall that at about the time that I went to grammar school, I had begun eating to excess, to the point of discomfort, especially before bedtime. My tummy would feel so uncomfortable, in fact, that no matter what position I lay in, I felt grossly nauseous. I knew then that I wasn't physically hungry but that I was feeling something else. All I could say was that I didn't really want all the food I was eating, but of course, to outsiders,

6

and to my parents, it seemed that I had a 'healthy appetite', which was almost applauded, and anyway, my mother told me I wouldn't be eating it if I didn't want it. Only now, in retrospect can I see that I was emotionally hungry, not physically hungry. The emotional void demanded love, talking, being listened to, as well as being heard, and being respected for my opinions; not biscuits, bread, cereal, cakes and food, food, unglorious food, unwanted food. The void felt like a huge black gaping hole – which, as the years rolled on, was to become a bottomless, even wider pit, and I experienced greater and greater isolation.

My first year at St Albans Girls Grammar School was horrid. The Beatles were the top pop group then, and a first question from one of my classmates was which Beatle and which song did I like most. I was stumped. I didn't even know who the Beatles were – only Children's Hour was allowed at home. We didn't have a television, and as much as I liked the wireless, it was not for popular, let alone pop music. I didn't have comics, either, except for *Look and Learn* because it was 'educational and good for you'.

I guess I started off secondary school life rather badly, but it only really compounded the isolation I had been feeling at home. I seemed to be a misfit everywhere. I tried latching on to fan-adulation of Paul McCartney and the Beatles' record *She loves you yeah, yeah, yeah*, but *no, no, no*, it didn't work; the Rolling Stones had come in, the pop circuit was changing rapidly and I was lost again, and lonely. 'Square' too now, because Beatlemania was old hat and I was out of date! I developed a few friends, but except for one dear one, Sandra, with whom I still keep contact, the rest was cupboard love. Sandra Hill (now Sandra Porter), stuck with, and by me, throughout, although perhaps even she didn't realise exactly what was going on. Unfortunately, as she gained some insight, so was she banned from visiting our house, as was Isobel Brown (too slovenly), Jenny Smith (too finicky), Rosemary McDonald (too untidy), Paul Minter (of Indian descent), Colin Humphrey (a Roman Catholic – we were Church of England), Mike Spiller (a rocker – a mod I think, but my father insisted he was a leather-jacketed rocker), Teresa Thorne (because she had a boyfriend, and 'was too young for such things'), and many, many others who were deemed 'common' and 'unsuitable'. I hated home-life. I left it as early as possible on schoolday mornings, and returned as late as possible. School was sometimes a sort of haven – I could hide in the locker-rooms – at other times it was the worst of the two evils because I was constantly being shown up by my peers – until I discovered I had a flair for most sports. I then started living for school; for the hockey, lacrosse, tennis and athletic matches and the gymnastics and dance lessons and competitions, but even that was slightly marred. Whatever my performance, it could have been better. The demand for perfectionism became my only goal in life. As far as home was concerned, I never achieved it (I can remember many a wallop and being sent to my room), and as far as school was concerned it was the same, because by now I was becoming my own judge and goal-setter too. I was unguardedly becoming my own worst enemy, echoing my father's demands and expectations. In my own eyes, now, I was never good enough. (Just as in later years I was never a good enough anorectic and I was never thin enough.) I felt an absolute failure, and was caught up in a wheel of despair, loneliness, desolation and isolation.

For a brief period, just after learning about sex, babies, and growing up, in the first form at school, I longed for a baby brother or sister. My longing became quite an obses-sion, and I so well remember the ache in the pit of my stomach of wanting that baby and trying to convey all my feelings to my parents. They, of course, thought I was 'being very silly', even though I earnestly promised that I would take full responsibility for doing everything for it! I yearned for someone to love (Billy my budgerigar was not enough), and, I think, believed that a baby brother or sister would put everything right for us as a family. Maybe my parents would love one another and at least the attention would be away from me. Also, I would be happy because I would be special – to my brother or sister. However, despite the tears which were almost tantamount to full-scale tantrums at times, as I tried to 'put my case', the answer was a definite no – because, as was suggested to me, such an event was expensive, both in terms of time and money, and would surely mean stopping all my ballet, horseriding, piano (and later, oboe) lessons. Oh what a pithy, pathetic excuse! But goodness, how I longed even more for the stork to come, when I heard that!

When I was about sixteen, however, there suddenly appeared a chance to be like my classmates, to join in with them and do something with them. Diet! Most of the girls I knew then were becoming very weight and figure conscious. They all wanted to be like Twiggy, and even though I thought this was my chance to prove I could be like them, I found an undercurrent of resentment. I can see why now – I *was* a Twiggy. A naturally very slender teenager who could eat anything and everything I wanted to, and who didn't need to lose weight. However, on to the bandwagon I jumped. For one this was a chance for me to exert some control over this seemingly insatiable night-time appetite (only insatiable, I think, because I could never fill up with what I didn't want), which had also started to creep in when I arrived home from school. My mother had started teaching, so now there was no-one in when I got home, and straight into our walk-in larder I would go, and just stand or crouch there, stuffing down great doorsteps of bread, butter and jam, and biscuits, and anything else that was quick and easy to hand. I felt a compulsion to have a taste of every damn thing in that larder; a shaving of cheese, so slight no-one would notice, a tiny slither of cake and ice cream, a finger dipped in the treacle and lemon curd, a swig of ketchup and a spoonful of salad cream, and oh, anything – the cream off the top of the milk, a handful of cereal! It didn't matter that the evening meal was only a couple of hours away, or that my tummy was hurting as it pushed and strained against my school-uniform skirt waistband and belt.

Strangely enough, I never seemed to gain any excess weight throughout this period, but between eleven and sixteen there had been a tremendous spurt of growth, and excelling in so many sports, so much of the time, meant I was very active. I also came of very slim stock, and was, as I say, naturally slim.

It was a ghastly place, that larder, but a hidey-hole in which to eat. If only I had realised how significant that secret eating was, and how significant, too, it was to become. However, as 'one of the crowd', I purchased some slimming aids (toffees which one ate after drinking a glass of water, preferably warm water), and to a degree – because I felt a little better now, doing the 'in thing' – managed to exert some sort of control. Not a lot though. You see, sweetwise, I had adored toffees as a child – and still did, so I rather over-indulged in those (without the water!). However, I was out of that horrid hidey-hole – the larder – but, again in retrospect, I suppose I was in another – my bedroom. The hidden slimming aids (my mother saw all this sort of thing as 'stuff and nonsense'), were ensconced and administered in my bedroom, in which I was now spending a lot of my time studying. There were hours and hours of homework leading up to my 'O' and 'A' levels, all of which I passed, but not without much worrying and anxiety. I was not a 'natural' when it came to exams; I had to work hard to pass and also it seemed to me as though I had been set yet another standard now. Prior to working, my mother had taken a teacher-training course, for which she needed to obtain a minimum of five 'O' levels. She gained them with flying colours. I came a poor second, when it came to comparing the grade of pass. HOWEVER, I did get some fairly good qualifications – nine 'O' levels, two 'A' levels, and a grade A 'AO' level in Human Biology.

Neither my family nor I were ever weight conscious. We were all slim and I didn't have a clue as to how much I weighed, despite the fact that we were regularly weighed at school, each new school year. I recall, around the age of fourteen, I think, my parents purchasing a pair of bathroom scales – on which to weigh our luggage. We were off on our first posh holiday abroad and my father was concerned that our luggage should be within the required weight limit. I think I got on the things – out of curiosity, but again they didn't mean anything, and I simply didn't register the reading; it was of no interest to me. Yet there was something wrong. Periods having only more or less started, stopped within eighteen months. They had been very irregular and for the length of time they were a part of my life, I had about five, possibly one or two more. Now, looking back yet again (as I do a lot in my book), I can see that the manifestation of dire need to control my intake of food was symptomatic of something far more sinister. It was really an effort to control my feelings and emotions and ignore that void. Quite possibly, the infrequency of my periods was indicative of my dis-ease. I was not in harmony; body, mind and soul were streets apart, lost in the black hole, the void.

> *A blackness, a void*
> *Like a great empty hole,*
> *I feel like a zombie,*
> *I've not got a soul.*
> *I can't win, I hate me*
> *I hate life and it's hell.*
> *Oh! Please let me sleep*
> *– but in a warm cosy shell.*
> *NOT 24 NEW GREENS AVENUE.*

(scribbled on one of my school scripture books in 1966)

Unfortunately, my parents were very strict (my view I know, which is naturally biased, but which, I am sure, is justified) and I felt I was living my life to please them. They treated me like a child in that I wasn't allowed to make any of my own decisions or voice my opinions, yet I could be treated as a totally responsible adult accountable for my own behaviour and attitudes. It was through these two extremes that I experienced an awful lot of internal conflict and my sense of feeling 'out of control'. I see, now, why that feeling surfaced. It is because when living at home, the power of parents' rules and wishes being a fact of life, they are very influential figures, so what they said or expected was not to be questioned. This sort of emotional abuse, like sexual abuse, especially in the formative years, can be as bad as one another, and can inflict great long-term damage. And, I think, it did.

When my periods started, my feelings of despair strengthened. They again brought out the childlike versus adult conflict and the implications of womanhood and femininity were something with which I could not cope easily. They also meant that even my body appeared to be 'out of control' and as all these inexpressed tensions built up, a release became vital. That release came with food and being constantly 'on the go', playing sport and exercising constantly. It was an attempt to solve the conflicts. I was not a well being, and I didn't have a sense of well-being; in moments of angry frustration I would try cutting myself with scissors, or my father's razor, but, frightened by physical pain at that age, I never managed anything more than sharp little cuts, despite wanting to do much more serious damage.

As a child and teenager, I was accountable to my parents, and to teachers. Growing up needing their approval as a symbol of their love, is quite normal, but it inevitably made for conflicts between meeting their needs and mine. I gradually began to believe that my parents were all that mattered and that I would not even fulfil my own basic need for food. I was internalising anger, shame, guilt and helplessness, and I hated myself and them – my mother and father.

In various bags and other portable carriers, I later carried a copy of a poem I'd found, written by Philip Larkin. It all seemed so sad, but if (as I felt my parents did), they blamed me, perhaps I could get some sort of consolation from being able to blame them a bit too. The snippet of the poem I kept with me reads thus:

> *They fuck you up, your Mum and Dad,*
> *They may not mean to, but they do.*
> *They fill you with the faults they had*
> *And add some extra just for you.*

The word 'fuck' leapt out at me; I felt fucked, I was being fucked about and I felt as ugly inside as this rather crude word conjures up, in the physical sense. Further, I was certain that my birth was the result of a violent act. Not love.

The void remaining, my 'dieting' got me nowhere. By the time I was eighteen, everything seemed worse. I was now about to go and train as a physical education teacher at Sussex University. At last I was leaving number 24, but this saw the start of the void becoming a greater bottomless pit. I was aware, too, of having chosen the same career as my mother – teaching – even though I had been intent on teaching PE since the word go, so there was more room for comparisons – and failure. Eating had not solved anything, being slim had not solved anything, trying to control my food intake had not solved anything. It had all got me nowhere. There was one thing left. Not eat. Starvation and emaciation were my new goals.

MY ANOREXIA

In the longing to be thin, nothing and no-one mattered now. Friends, family, lovers, were all at the mercy of my obsession. In less than half a year I remember dropping from eight stone twelve pounds, (I had started weighing myself), to somewhere between three and a half and four stones, around which I hovered for the next twenty years, except for the many hospital admissions when I was force-fed to raise my weight a little. (When I was discharged, or discharged myself, I made sure I lost that extra weight very quickly.) Four stones seemed 'safe', but it didn't last long. The perfectionist in me set higher standards; ie, lower weights. It was, I can see now, an all-out effort to punish myself as harshly as possible, probably to justify all the guilt and hurt I felt inside. Kill or cure just didn't come into it. There was no room for logic. I *had* to be thin – thinner – and as the weight dropped lower, I experienced a kind of euphoric 'buzz'. An energy that somehow allowed me to go on living and a 'buzz' that gave me a peculiar sense of excitement. I had no idea why I wanted to be thin and/or thinner – I just did – but I was euphoric, on a sort of high, and I kept aiming for impossibly low target weights.

Having at this point, as I've mentioned earlier, now earned the label 'anorectic', (which I firmly denied), for the first five years I was a walking calorie-counter, and exerted rigid discipline on both food and fluid intake. I was completely obsessed about what I was and wasn't going to eat and how and when. The small amounts I allowed myself, I ate slowly. I wanted to savour everything; it wasn't going to last long and I was hungry really, although I wouldn't admit that to myself, let alone to anyone else. (Anorexia nervosa is not one dictionary definition of 'nervous loss of appetite', it is wanton denial of hunger and food). When that pleasure ended, I felt guilty, I was a fat greedy pig, and I was fatter. I shouldn't have eaten, I must exercise it off – and not eat again for at least the next three days. I latched on to 'safe foods' – cottage cheese, apples, one-calorie diet Coke, natural yoghurt and half a fish cake. (At first I justified this 'cutting down' on my intake, by becoming a vegetarian first of all, then a vegan. And then every Lent I would give up some other foods.) However, I carried the torment further. I would be on and off the weighing scales at least twenty times daily and every morning I would look at myself in the mirror. How many bones could I count? Were my hip bones protruding enough? Could I still see each rib, count each vertebra? Every bone had to stick out and the rest of me sink in. My tummy had to be concave. Nothing else would do; otherwise the panic would set in. I also had 'safe' clothes – another torment. No elastic waistbands for me – even if I wore a baggy overtop. Everything had to fit just so; if it felt tight, I was scared – I was fat, if loose I was ecstatic – I was thinner, and would then alter the clothes to make them smaller – setting myself up, of course, for further anxiety. What if they didn't fit tomorrow?

My bones even had to show through thick clothing and the tape measure was out constantly, measuring every part of me, at two or three-hourly intervals, to make sure there was no increase; ie, no fat. A weigh-in in one part of the room wasn't good enough; I'd move the scales around the room, to see if I could get a lower reading. (I recall on one occasion, convincing myself that no floor in my flat was level, so I took the scales onto the pavement outside, wearing the minimum amount of clothing to be decent – which of course I had also weighed in order to know exactly how much *I* weighed.) And when I did, I still wasn't satisfied! I was suspicious of the scales not working properly, and the floors, and every lump and bump there might be. I'd then run from chemist to chemist to find the real truth, but I could never find it – all the public scales gave a different reading, a different weight. But! Maybe I'd run off a few more ounces in that panic attack, and it was with that sense of 'betterness' I returned home. Maybe, just maybe, I was lighter and thinner...

This mental torture having gone on through my university years (where I again felt the odd one out), went with me to my first job as a physical education teacher at Roedean. I was, as far as I was concerned, failing all the time, and therefore a failure. I hated myself more and more. Self-confidence, self-esteem and self-respect were almost at an all-time low. (As the years went on the 'all-time' lows got lower and lower. Goodness knows the real low!) Many of the pupils had a crush on me, and I wasn't short of boyfriends, but I often wondered why. How could anyone possibly like me? But sometimes the compliments would boost me a little, enough to come in to the daylight and have some social contact. However, feeling I had nothing to contribute in this field, I would dress up very smartly, and emphasise my very slim figure, thin figure, emaciated figure. And for a while it would last. Heads would turn and people showed signs of envy regarding my sixteen inch waist. They also admired my 'large, beautiful eyes', but there was something else, and it was only on hearing of Ray Moore's one meeting with Karen Carpenter that I could put my finger on it.

A few years back now, Ray spoke of Karen being 'beautiful, with haunted eyes', and 'bewitching' – having a beauty which was emphasised the more so by her 'fragile vulnerability'. I cried when I heard this because my eyes had also often been described as 'almost haunted' making me, too, it seemed fragile and vulnerable, which for some signified beautiful. But that description gave away for more. I *was* haunted, haunted by fear. People looking at me were not seeing beauty, they were seeing fear. If only they had known and if only I could have told them. My fragile vulnerability was emphasised because of my size, but to some people it was obviously seen as a form of beauty/attraction. If only

16

they could have seen this differently. Karen Carpenter died shortly after that meeting with Ray Moore – from anorexia nervosa, which up until her death, had gone unrecognised by many.

On the other side of the fence were the people who considered thinness to be ugly and vulgar, and when cries of 'Have you just walked out of Belsen or something?' came, I ran away to hide. WHAM! I was back in the gutter with an even more urgent and chronic need to kick myself further into it, if possible:

> *Like a snake I recoil.*
> *I'm vicious, it's harsh.*
> *I'm disgusting, quite vile –*
> *I should live in a marsh.*
> *A bog's more precise*
> *I could lie like the filth,*
> *Disgusting and horrid*
> *Stinking black, like the silt.*

(written on a scrap of paper in February 1979).

At some stage in all this, and all I remember is that it was in that first job, I began to realise this wanting to be slim was *not* just about the deadly pursuit of thinness, which I had managed to convince myself it was. Terrified, I knew there was something far more to it, but was too lost in the physical symptoms. Just what could it all be about? I knew that I wanted to be popular, be liked – by everyone – be loved, be a leader, be the life and soul of the party, be successful, ie, be PERFECT, but I felt mentally detached from my body sometimes, as though there was a VOICE inside, dictating what I should and should not do. And craftily, by way of thinking in this way, I began to refer to my anorexia as a Voice, a Demon, a Devil, another part of me. I was a victim of a devil (anorexia nervosa was not of *my* doing or choosing), all I had to do was kill it. I didn't, or perhaps wouldn't, accept my anorexia as a part of *me*. Albeit unwittingly,

17

though, this eating disorder *was* my choice; my way of communicating with the world and myself that I was emotionally unwell. And my way too, of suppressing strong emotions. However, I saw it now as something I could get rid of – any time I wanted to, and thus I actually so allowed myself to continue to be ill. My thought patterns, my anorectic behaviour and my mind were very devious! I pulled the wool over even my own eyes. Once, when sitting on the toilet experiencing severe diarrhoea one end, and vomiting the other, into a bucket, cramps attacking my shins, feet, hands, stomach and chest, I still vividly remember promising myself that this was the last time. Tomorrow I'd stop, I'd be better. But tomorrow never came ...

Not only was I scared stiff of food, I was, more or less, scared stiff of everything: situations, relationships (professional or personal), and living, so in frantic moments I'd run to a place of privacy and strip off my clothes, look at my body, and if I was a bit thinner, if I'd lost a bit more weight, then I was OK. For a few hours at least. At times it seemed that being thin gave me confidence, but that was how I was kidding myself. I could do anything and everything if I was thin, and indeed I held down good careers for seventeen years. Yet the inside me and the outside me were giving off mixed messages: 'I can do anything, but if I don't manage it, it's because I'm so small and fragile. I'm frail and thin, be gentle and careful with me. Don't get cross or shout, or get angry and be demanding. I'm not like you, I'm unwell, I need careful loving,' was the message I gave to the world, whilst inside I felt shitty and fat and gross and ugly. I think, now, the latter part of the message said it all. I needed everyone to know I was in a mess. Anger, hurt, shouting and demanding behaviour, were all too reminiscent of childhood years. I wanted the world to share my hurt, yet I couldn't tell them. I could only communicate its extent by my painful appearance, which, unfortunately was simply referred to as the 'slimmer's disease'. Something 'very silly' and 'self-imposed'. My fault.

What do you really see
When you look at me?
– just a very thin girl?
God! my mind's in a whirl.
Do you ever wonder about me inside?
'Cos really I'm desperately wanting to hide.
I'm crying, I'm screaming,
I'm calling for help,
But I feel you don't love me or care how I feel,
– or if you do, you just give me a meal.
I don't want it!
I don't need it!
My life is a hell.
– it doesn't seem real, curled up in a shell.
I'm angry, I'm guilty, ashamed of myself,
I hate me, too – but you?
Please can't you see –
I need to know that somebody cares,
Instead of feeling that everyone stares.
Please ask of me how I really am,
Give me a chance to tell you about this sham.
And when I've done that, please try and see
That I long to be normal – be a real person –ME.

(1981 diary)

Although I have referred to my equating thinness with
success, I also longed to be like other people, normal. Fat,
thin, whatever, they all seemed to be enjoying themselves,
they managed life, they were happy. If only I could be like
them and eat. Hamburgers, chips, ice cream and all the other
food stuffs, eat those things just like them and not think
anything of it. I must have asked the same old question a
million times over: 'Why can't I be normal like everyone else,
and eat without worrying?'

Sometimes I felt strong enough to vow that I would. I'd
stop all this stupidity around food. I would eat properly,
starting tomorrow, and I'd be well. Caught up in the all-

19

consuming obsession with food, weight, shape and size, I too thought being normal was eating properly. Only now – now that I have recovered – can I look back and see how dreadfully wrong I was, and understand why, if that was the case, I couldn't simply eat and not be scared to. Freedom from anorexia – or any eating disorder, does, certainly, involve eating properly, but that is *not* what it's all about. It means being free to hang on to your feelings and express them. (Free now, as I am, to express my emotions, be they sad, happy, or angry, whether I be laughing, crying or having fun, puts me in touch with me, and I feel OK in this freedom of expression, no longer hating myself. The self-confidence, self-respect, and self-esteem are very high on the slide rule these days!) If only I could have seen that – then. Instead when my tomorrows came, I did eat properly – so I kidded myself, in a controlled way, (very controlled), which meant eating three times a day, but no more than one cup of black coffee, half an apple and a third of a pot of cottage cheese each time. I did not realise my need to control – control everything i.e. my feelings, my food, my relationships and my life – was such an important issue, because inside my head, I felt right out of control even though every thought I had seemed, because of my ill state, to be completely logical. I didn't trust myself. I would still take my laxatives and diuretics, and vomit – just in case I'd got fatter, or just in case I ate a bit more than I should. The sheer disciplined control I had been exercising on my food intake in the first few years had slipped a little and it was totally by accident that I discovered vomiting, and, later, laxatives and diuretics. My fears had been calmed and my prayers answered: I *could* eat – and still lose weight! But all it really signified was the onset of even more pretence and a bigger sham.

In reality, then, as my tomorrow never came, it never will for others. Not I, nor anyone, is in control of their eating disorder. Willpower is not the answer. It is a recovery process that demands time, help and maybe therapy in order to examine the underlying issues behind the behavioural and emotional problems. It demands a change in the way you think about yourself and the way in which you feel others see you and it also demands letting go such disciplined control – maybe handing over a little to others – and trusting – oneself and others. Such scary thoughts!

My anorexia, at the stage when I kidded myself I could eat 'properly', was my enemy and a liar; I was doing nothing other than exerting more rigid control over my feelings and emotions. I, of course, thought I just had great will power, and got a morbid sense of self-satisfaction and achievement that those few tomorrows offered. But then the tomorrows went haywire, and paradoxically, it showed me to be in even less control. I was so scared of myself. I was a liar to myself. I couldn't see the truth and I wanted to run away from my anorexia. But the Voice used to tell me I'd be OK. And I believed it, or did I?

BELIEVE ME

'Take heart, be strong', the Voice says,
'You're fine as you are.
You can be one of them
– the people you see –
Whenever you want. You're OK.'

'Believe me, I know', the Voice says,
'You're fine, like the others.
You are one of them
– the people you see –
All the time. You're OK.'

'You can join in', the Voice says,
'Just like everyone else.
Be a part of the world
– the people you see –
Anytime you wish. You're OK.'

'It's scary out there', I say, though,
'I'm useless, I'm different.

I can't be part of that place
– the people I see –
Ever. No, I'm not OK.'

'Stay then, in prison', the Voice says,
'It's cosy, you're warm.
And maybe none has the key
– the people you see –
To freedom. Stay here. OK?'

Obviously, my dramatic weight-loss prompted many questions from both my family and friends. Some were kind, some offered help (food!), some were quite brutal, but they were all an attempt to get me to 'pull up my socks and eat properly'. Initially I had avoided eating with people, because I didn't want them to see how little I ate, but when it became obvious I didn't look well, I started the lying again – to myself and to others. I invented all sorts of reasons for losing weight: hormones, kidneys, liver, bowel difficulties – whatever I could think of. I even tried telling people that I was just one of those lucky people who could eat anything and everything but just couldn't put on weight! I had such a super-duper metabollic rate! Then to prove my point, I would eat with them – or at least appear to. Beforehand, I'd take a mega dose of laxatives, and always wore clothes with pockets. When it came to the meal, I took one of three options: as every mouthful went up to, or into, my mouth, so I would blow my nose, and spit the food into my hanky. Sometimes I was actually able to whisk the food off my plate on to my lap. (Oh, the amount of gravy and other stains I had to account for!) Or I did really chew it and swallow it. Quite often it was a combination of all three. Then, as the meal finished, I would leave the table, pockets bulging with hankies and serviettes full of food, and go into an adjoining room and vomit – into the plastic bags I carried with me especially for the purpose. Going to the toilet after every meal would have been far too obvious, and anyway vomiting was quite an easy, simple thing to do. I could do it

22

silently and without putting my fingers down my throat. It didn't seem to matter at that point how difficult a problem it might be getting rid of those bags of vomit; I just had to get rid of the food, and anyway, I always did manage to engineer a sneaking-out plan, regarding the bags.

I was so devious, and I hated myself, the more so for this, perhaps. Where was it getting anyone, least of all me? Just making the dance with death a *danse macabre*, an aeonic *pas seul*. Somewhat ironic, this analogy with dance, because gymnastics and dance had always been my forte, and what I had enjoyed best. But then perhaps that was part of it. I was not allowed to enjoy (anything) any more, so dancing and food were horrible and terrifying. I was dancing to kill myself now; self-abuse and self-punishment were the rulers, and the Voice was swift to kill anything that might allow pleasure. For example, as I moved on from job to job (following Roedean, I left the teaching profession – I felt too lonely – and entered the office world, gaining posts in senior administration), instead of celebrating promotion in a fun way, I would take a party dose of laxatives – to hurt myself, to get thinner, perhaps, and to deny myself any feelings of pleasure or satisfaction.

In contrast to the hurt the purging caused, I also derived a macabre pleasure from it and would often look forward gleefully to the next day following a purge. Then I felt so ill and weak – and it was wonderful. The pain in my head, any feelings or emotions, were all taken away and no matter the acute shortage of breath, the distorted hearing, the inability to stand upright to walk and the devastating weakness, I was safe for a while. Everything was on hold.

During all this time I never actually questioned why this was happening to me, or what I had done to deserve it. Even at my worst, I think I knew, I think I was aware, that I had subconsciously *chosen* this way of coping with life. I had chosen to get very thin, and stay thin. But I couldn't understand why; the Voice would tell me I was shitty, hateful, and deserved all this. Fearing the battles with the Voice, I asked no further questions. I quietly resigned myself to this life –

this existence, a starve-purge-vomit machine that did whatever the Voice demanded.

I had also chosen to be on my own in the early years, mainly to avoid social contacts that inevitably involved eating. (This being on my own was a reproduction, I feel, of my childhood years.) I had felt the world to be my enemy – they were wrong, I didn't have anorexia nervosa, but now I knew *I* was wrong. My chronic denial had brought desperate loneliness. I could no longer choose to be on my own, I had dropped all my friends and contacts, and some of them me. I *had* to be on my own. And with the fear I was experiencing, being on my own was terrifying. I was now lonely. I thought death was the only way out and made many serious all-out suicide bids. I became a regular at the local intensive care unit. Yet, for some reason I went on surviving. Several times I was found too late for stomach-pumping, yet a dose of 150 Paracetamol (taken, I'm afraid, on several occasions – once on the beach in Brighton, where I spent a few days and nights in an unconcious state), did nothing to me. No liver damage was incurred either, and if at any point in this book I thank my mother, it is now. I must have had the constitution of an ox to survive all that I did to myself! Even if it was done begrudgingly, she got me off to a sound start, and she always baked very wholesome food. Meals were very nutritious. As a child, I suffered very, very, few colds, and only had the chicken pox. Likewise, during the years I had my eating disorder, I again seemed to have my own inbuilt immune system; coughs, colds, flu, stomach viruses, I avoided them all. Quite why, I'm not sure, because one would think that, being in such a poor state of health, I would fall foul of anything. However, one theory that may pinpoint the reason (although I am aware many anorectics are very prone to, and *do* go down with many viruses and bugs), is that the body develops its own defence mechanism, by practically closing down everything. All its energies are needed to concentrate on keeping the vital organs going, in order to go on living and breathing, not fighting contagious diseases.

My starvation had a powerful affect on others – much more than talking, crying, getting angry, 'having tantrums', etc. But the power behind refusing food, and getting thinner, was *self*-destructive, as well as destroying everything else. There was no end, and as far as everyone else was concerned, 'eating properly' and 'building yourself up' was the answer, so the more I ate the better. I would be strong and healthy! My silence became greater instead; there did not seem to be any listening or sympathetic ears. Perhaps it was an angry response to people's attitudes that sent me on the downhill slope of all those vast quantities of laxatives, diuretics and suppositories. The pain they caused was extreme and it was a vicious, angry thing to do, to inflict such discomfort, as was vomiting every time I ate or drank – sometimes making my throat bleed, on purpose.

Unless you have suffered anorexia nervosa, it is impossible for you to really understand and appreciate the euphoric 'buzz' that comes from days of starvation: a euphoria also created by sheer exhaustion from the purging, vomiting, and starving – with the 'excited' feeling that weight-loss brings – as well as imposing upon oneself vigorous exercise routines, such as a hundred sit-ups every other hour. Nor might you be able to understand the sheer pleasure and sensation of relief, caused by a good vomiting and purging session. I felt so clean and pure inside – until it started again. Sometimes I drank diluted bleach in order to get out the filth I felt inside. However you might be able to understand why I kept silent. Why I felt ashamed. Why I felt I couldn't tell you about these disgusting, yet compulsory things. Not understanding it myself, I used silence, too, as a coping mechanism, but of course, this meant the circle kept turning. I was a prisoner of my eating disorder:

> *I can see you,*
> *And you can see me.*
> *I realise that this is*
> *No place to be, and*
> *Sometimes I long to*

Break free from my Prison.
I want somebody to help me,
Won't anybody – please?
The prison bars are between us,
Where are the keys?
You can't reach me
I can't let you in.
I'll have to go on
– serving this sentence in Prison.

('To the World' – August 1980).

Although my anorexia was always recognised as a psychiatric, rather than a physical problem – and I was sectioned many times by the medical authorities – it only seemed to be the intrinsic symptoms that were treated; ie, the depression, sleeplessness, inbalances in blood, etc, and weight-loss. All were treated via medication and the dreaded thing called food, although sometimes my condition being a life-threatening one, I would be given an intravenous and naso-gastric tube. On these occasions I remember lying flat on my back on the bed, and watching the drips – drip, drip, drip, fatter, fatter, fatter – and I would yank the things out, terrified, only to have them re-inserted, and my arms taped to the bed. Occasionally though, through what must be recognised as an amazing feat of contortions, I still managed to disconnect myself, and once a tube was inserted into my stomach instead. A very unpleasant experience.

There was no looking beyond my body and food, no looking at the me inside. Occasionally, when the medics asked me 'Why?' all I could say was 'I don't know. I hate myself,' and it was left there. There just didn't seem to be a key to unlock what was now a prison cell, in which I felt I was serving a sentence of solitary confinement. All that mattered was hurting and abusing myself, and being thin, despite the fact that it was already a horror story. I was losing all of my hair. Pubic and underarm hair had ceased to grow. Instead hair was developing over my back, shoulders and face – called Lanugo hair – in an effort to keep my body warm. I no longer perspired – I needed to keep the heat in, and I was always cold. Most of my teeth had fallen out and my eye-sight was blurred. My hearing was affected by a constant rushing sound and my bottom lip and the sides of my mouth were badly split, often bleeding. I was forever suffering cramps over the whole of my body, including my shins, thighs, hands and toes, stomach and chest. Sometimes these attacks would last half an hour or more, and I would scream in agony – into a cushion or pillow so that my neighbours would not hear. I experienced, too, breathing difficulties, and my heartbeat became irregular (laxatives strip the body of potassium and magnesium, two trace elements upon which the heart relies in order to function). My blood pressure was very, very low and my heartbeat very, very slow, yet I still went on (miraculously) living. But, as the next decade approached and I continued to exist, the prison sentence became worse... Bingeing began. And bulimia nervosa.

MY BINGEING AND BULIMIA NERVOSA

Some people who have anorexia nervosa merely restrict their diet and thereby remains their control. However, after a decade of doing just that, except for occasional 'slip-ups', I started bingeing as well. Those 'slip-ups', I could see at the time, were reinforced by my low weight and inadequate and irregular food intake. I remember one vivid occasion when I was at university, deciding one morning that I was going to completely abstain from all foods and fluids for three days (a three-day *raison d'etre*, I suppose), and thus threw myself into my work, spending as much time as possible in the library. However, towards the end of the second day I felt an uncontrollable urge to eat. It had to be in secret, no-one I knew seeing me, hence I had to go to the local shopping area. A three mile bicycle trip. I cycled there in a mad frenzy and remember purchasing an Aztec bar which I shovelled in as I made my return. But I couldn't return – I wanted another and another and another. And so I did. I felt very guilty, ashamed and nauseous on that homebound cycle ride, which was peppered with stops at several chemists to buy a punishing dose of laxatives, and worse still I was already making rules about not eating or drinking anything again – this time it had to be for six days. Double punishment! The greater the punishment the more often I would succeed, though. It was a hard battle, but an inevitable one – my body was obviously reacting to starvation with increased preoccupation with food and hunger, and sometimes I could not resist it. When I failed to, of course, I felt as though my control had snapped and I had to inflict greater punishments to re-instate it.

28

I refer to these episodes as 'slip-ups' because in my early anorectic years a binge to me constituted a very small amount, ie, anything over and above what I was allowed, or rather what *I* was allowing *myself*. And I think this is the case for many anorectics: two tubs of cottage cheese instead of just half, two apples instead of one, and anything fatty or carbohydrate was a binge. However, as the second decade of my eating disorder began, so bingeing took on a totally different concept.

Exactly when the excessive eating of anything and everything (usually carbohydrates and sugary and gooey foods) began, is difficult to pinpont. It was obvious to me, I suppose, even at that point, that severe limitation of intake and attacks of self-abuse and punishment were not getting me anywhere. The euphoric buzz was disappearing. My body seemed to have adjusted itself to its low weight, and I could feel strong emotions surfacing again. Even though they all seemed to be about food, shape, size and weight, and when I would and would not eat, anger, hurt, despair and fear were strong and they were very distressing and frightening in themselves. I remember praying to God to give me back my will-power to not eat, and for a while became an earnest church-goer in order that God might grant me that favour! But it appeared that He chose not to. He hated me too! So for a brief while I sought alternative forms of medication. Acupuncture and hypnosis in particular, as well as aromatherapy, yoga and meditation. But they all failed to help. (Not surprising perhaps – because I never disclosed my eating disorder; I would always visit under the guise of some other problem, for example, sleeplessness, or constant feelings of nausea and unable to relax.) Then, for a period of about six months (I had been doing part-time work as a barmaid since student days), I turned to alcohol. Three or four bottles of wine a day, with, when on duty, an immeasurable amount of shorts, or rather longs – tumblers full of vodka. Come the evenings I was blotto – in the true sense of the word. All feelings and emotions were blotted out, but I got myself into a worse predicament. I was constantly wetting and soiling the bed. With very little food inside me, and all those purgatives, it was hardly surprising. Many a night was spent sleeping in a stinking bed. A bed that went on stinking even after a change of linen, because it was a divan, and the stains soaked right through the base.

All this, of course, lowered my self-esteem even further. I was past the gutter now, I'd travelled down the drains and was floating sewage. To add to my almost non-existent self-esteem, I had also begun to shoplift. At first it was because I simply didn't have enough money to support my habit – now extending beyond purgatives, diuretics, and suppositories, to alcohol and food, as well as afford a mortgage, car and other household bills. It also expressed that low self-esteem. I hated myself so much that in a way this confirmed the hateful person I felt I was: 'I'm a terrible person. I even steal'.

Oh God! – the agony of knowing what I do
– just what my conscience screams out not to.
I'm a split personality.
Though one side cares – my conscience,
The other wants destruction, cell by cell, nerve by
*   nerve.*
So I carry on whilst others think 'how nice', 'how
*   pleasant'.*
If only they knew – I'm not.
– If only they or I understood,
If they just scratched the surface they would find
*   me*
– a devil, a demon with a hell-scorched soul.
One who wants and needs and yet stoops so low.
But it's my fault, I'm to blame
I chose this torture, to live apart from life
– and love.
To steal instead, and hate – everything.
Always taking it out on myself and what I eat.
Yes! I'm to blame for what has become of who I am.

(1980 diary)

Over the years, stealing also served two other purposes. Firstly, it distracted me from eating (I rarely stole food), whilst I thrived on the heady excitement I sensed with regard to what I was about to, or what I had, done. And secondly (and I would like to point out nothing I took was of much value), I just loved to accumulate. Even if, as was mostly the case, I was not going to use any of my amassed 'goodies', just to see them and experience that sense of achievement was enough.

Other behavioural patterns had also started to creep in which became obsessional routines, mainly involving cleanliness and neatness. I became a slave to the rituals of my addiction, which monopolised my early morning and evening home life. I felt unable to leave my flat in the morning until all my self-imposed chores were completed. To do so would only mean dreadful feelings of guilt and frustration which would eat away at me – and I started to eat back, ie, physically. Binges became more frequent, and I started to consume larger amounts. The need for cleanliness became worse then, too. Every time I ate and then vomited, I had to wash all the clothes I was wearing at the time. And me! An attempt to wash all the badness away. Bingeing frequently each day resulted in a great deal of washing. Yet more bills to meet – visits to the launderette. I can remember the sheer frustration on one occasion being so marked that I decided to just shove all my 'dirty' clothes in the bath to soak – perhaps out of all this would come some good. If all my clothes were in soak, I wouldn't be able to go out – to buy food, to steal, to get laxatives and purgatives. I'd be in control of it all! It never worked though – I always had something to wear – a mac over my nightie or underclothes. Or, as on more than one occasion, I 'found' something. An old coat, an old shirt kept for decorating, for example.

I had begun to feel that I was now paying a very high price for being ill and trying to recover. At least that is what I thought I was doing – trying to recover, but my 'recovery process' was only by way of finding distractions or developing obsessions and routines. Anything to stop thinking about food! And naturally the harder I tried to stop thinking about food, the more I did, so the binges became more frequent, but not very large amounts each time, although enough to make my nightmare even more terrifying. The boat was starting to rock. I had lost the ability to just starve myself. I could sense an oncoming storm, and in my desperation to avoid it, I got married, on 9th December 1980.

That first marriage, to Ray, lasted eight months. I knew the moment I signed the register I had made a dreadful mistake, and oh, the feeling in the pit of my stomach was indescribable! Our marriage was never consummated – hardly surprising. At four stones one's libido is not there, nor at five stones to which weight I had binged to 'look better' for my wedding day (knowing I could quickly lose it). Also, Ray, being in the licensing trade, had more than a healthy interest in drink. Although the marriage ended in bitterness, and I blamed myself, I think it only fair to say that it was a marriage of convenience for both of us. I remember thinking if I had somebody else to care for and live for (I did not realise at first the extent of Ray's alcohol addiction), I would get better. Everything would be all right. Love would solve everything. As for Ray, maybe he thought the same (although he, too, did not have a clue as to the extent of my problems). We never really discussed it – either because he was drunk or I was in a numbed state following mass laxative doses after vomiting. I certainly did not look upon marriage as a relationship, a responsibility. I simply saw it as the answer to solving everything.

Violent arguments and aggressive behaviour ensued. Ray started to demand a sex life and we often had fights, and I for my part became much more devious and secretive. Going to the toilet to vomit or have diarrhoea left a lingering suspicious smell, and I couldn't always eat when I wanted to or needed to. Fortunately his publican's hours meant Ray was away most evenings and weekends, and he would have a meal at work, but I was vomiting and purging in buckets, saucepans and carrier bags – into anything which I could hide. One morning however when Ray got up – in a somewhat benevolent mood, even after a heavy night's drinking, he offered to do some washing up. As he bent under the sink to open the cupboard for some washing-up liquid, he was greeted with the stench of a bucketful of vomit and diarrhoea I had had to hide suddenly – and subsequently forgotten. I shouted at him to leave, I felt so ashamed, but I was also inwardly angry. I had discovered our bank balance to be zilch. Ray's addiction was costly too, and something I could not deal with. I was frightened as well because it was just like a scenario from childhood days. To everyone outside no. 24 my father was a most charming and helpful person, but behind closed doors he was entirely different. Likewise Ray – and me! Ray had many friends and was a great conversationalist, able to talk about most things and appeared to have a very kind and caring nature. In our relationship it was completely different. I felt it had to be my fault. I felt I was driving him to drink and because of that guilt, I punished myself more within the realms of my eating disorder. I felt I had destroyed two lives, although I was equally aware of Ray's devious behaviour too – drinking secretly (the tell-tale smell on his breath) and draining our savings. Perhaps if we hadn't married he would have been well and happy. I hope his scars were not too deep from the time we spent together. I never meant or intended to purposely hurt anyone, only myself.

With the distress of my marriage and its subsequent dissolution and the divorce, I turned more and more to food, and at one point, possibly because of the trauma, found I could eat quite a lot of food, and without vomiting (I was too tired) but still purging, still lose weight. I remember endless nights of getting up to make buttered toast, going backwards and forwards to the kitchen to make more to bring it back to eat in the comfort of a warm cosy bed, curtains drawn, lights out, no-one seeing or hearing. And then getting up again... And I think it was somewhere at this stage that the gasket blew and the storm really began, making the aforesaid rocking of my boat seem just like a gentle cradling motion. I started eating horrendous quantities of food. I was swinging from a famine to a feast. Although everything was real it was also like a dream, but a horrid one, the nightmare of which I have spoken. It seemed dreamlike because of the self-protective mechanism which was in play, enabling me to survive (of sorts), and I think this is true because things only became real when I finally worked through the pains of my experiences in my final hospital admission, years later, in 1989. (There I determined to set out on the road to recovery, and found I could survive as a whole, feeling being, who knew the value of life and its scars.)

By now, instead of keeping the cupboards and fridge-freezer bare, I was stocking them to capacity. I was starting to hoard food. There had, in the past, been embarrassing occasions when friends or visitors called and I had nothing to offer them, so I kidded myself that this was for them and not me. Hence the cupboards and fridge-freezer remained stocked – it *was* for them after all! If I wanted anything I had to go out and get it. The hoarding was fast becoming a compulsive habit. Whenever I broke into 'their' food, I had to go out immediately to replace it. But this discipline didn't last long either. At night I would torment myself about all the goodies I could stuff. In an effort to forget them I took mass doses of medication I'd been prescribed, but this led to worse things. Sometimes I felt what I can only describe as a presence at the end of my bed – that's all I can remember. Many mornings I stumbled out of bed to find that, without consciously knowing it, I had binged in the night. The evidence was on the kitchen floor – half empty tins of pasta, beetroot, unsteamed steamed puddings. Often there were remains of cheese, ice cream and ready-to-eat frozen meals too. I had raided the freezer, without realising it. I'd eaten things raw and/or rock hard. It seemed I had eaten them all off the floor, too, like an animal. I'd find stains on my nightie, on the bed linen, and many many times I found I'd broken a tooth. Presumably it broke when biting into the frozen food. My dentist had already replaced all my own lost teeth with caps and bridges, and I was now breaking these regularly. I looked like a witch with broken teeth and teeth missing. I felt like that evil presence at the end of the bed. When I plucked up the courage I visited the dentist, but I was fast running out of excuses as to why I needed all this dental repair work. Biting into an apple or a raw carrot without thinking could only be an excuse for two or three occasions! And I was incurring further monetary outlay again. I felt that either I *was* a witch – out of *Macbeth* – or there was a witch casting a spell on me. That presence was scary beyond words:

> *Somebody's there at the end of the bed*
> *Crouching and laughing, who wickedly said*
> *'Go eat all that food*
> *It will do in your head.*
> *Go on – stuff it down,*
> *– it* might *do some good –*
> *You can always come back,*
> *And hide, wearing my hood.'*

> *A witch with a laugh then took up the stance*
> *Cackling with glee she'd invite me to dance,*
> *'There's goodies galore,*
> *Come on, eat them all*
> *Enjoy them, it's fun,*
> *We'll dance well at this ball*
> *And if at the end you tire, don't you see*
> *– there's always tomorrow*
> *And chocolate gâteaux for tea'.*

(1984 diary)

Exactly at what point my bingeing meant I was suffering bulimia nervosa I do not know, but I don't think labels to be very important. All I do know is that I was feeling doubly worse. OK, people could see I was unwell – I was painfully thin, and remained so, even at those 'safe' four stones, throughout the bulimic years, but they thought I wasn't eating. Some people even envied my superb will-power in this respect (mainly people who themselves were overweight), but if only they knew this other side of me now. This stuffing, bingeing, purging, vomit machine, this fat, greedy, vile pig. But how could I tell them? How could I tell them it wasn't so much a physical hunger as an attempt, this time, to stuff back down any feelings that might come welling up? Unlike in my teenage years when eating had been an attempt to fill up the huge emotional void I felt.

When I discovered that as well as death through starvation, there was the possibility of death from a binge, I perked up a little, and soon became positively delighted. Maybe I *could* die. Maybe God would have no choice but to let me go. Starvation and overdoses hadn't worked, nor had walking blindly into roads in front of traffic, and driving my car like a lunatic, twice, into a brick wall. (On both occasions the cars were write-offs, but me, no, I walked away, without even a bruise!) So the bingeing became worse still, although I can see now that it was also acting as a safety valve. My body in the early stages of my bulimia, anyway, was crying out for food. It was starving. And to a degree I was meeting its needs/demands; I answered the call. But I felt so guilty afterwards I had to purge and vomit.

Subsequently then, from wanting initially to live as a slim/thin/emaciated person (labelled an 'anorectic'), I now wanted, with all my heart to die, and that in the last five years, from 1984–1989, became my ultimate goal. My bingeing and starving cycle, vomiting and purging, and shoplifting worsened. How well I remember crouching in front of the fridge, sometimes in the early hours, sometimes when I arrived home from work, getting ready to stuff down all the contents – and perhaps die from heart failure as my body tried to cope with all this intake, or choke on my own vomit as I tried to bring it all back. I remember too, the occasions when I baby-sat (to earn extra, much needed, income) I would raid their food sources, eating some there, and taking some home for a later, secret gorge. At the same time, the feelings of guilt were becoming compounded by the disorder itself – I had now reached the stage of having little control over my bladder and bowels. Often I was incontinent and soiled myself whilst out in public. I was REVOLTING, DISGUSTING – a PIG:

Snort, snuffle, stink
Head in trough
Head in sink.
Shove it all in
Then let it all out,
Down between your legs
Or out through your mouth.

You're nothing but horrid,
No woman's like this,
You are though,
You are just like piss.
Go put your head
Back in the trough.
You'll never, never, EVER EVER have enough.

Enough of what?
What you don't really want?
You're a disturbed mental lot
Like dirt in a font.
You're nothing but shit,
So go mould the wood
get into your coffin
You should – IF YOU FIT.

(Written 1986, 2.00am one morning in May. I weighed just under four stones, but felt, after a hefty session of gorging the previous day, like Billy Bunter).

I always seemed to hear the Voice before a binge, now telling me to go out, get food: 'Don't worry. You can always vomit it up and purge it out', it would say, and out I would go. I had to get and eat the food as quickly as possible when the Voice told me to binge. It was a frenzy of activity. I would literally run into a supermarket, grabbing anything I could – biscuits, cakes, bread, soft creamy cheese, half pound packets of butter, which I would eat like an ice cream, tins of gooey pasta and cans of fizzy drinks, and so much more. The store's shopping basket (and later trolley), would be loaded. I would start eating the food as I shopped and woe betide if the queue was a long one – the need to binge was too urgent and I would shoplift the lot, along with my usual 200 laxatives, and now (incurring yet more expense), feminine body colognes and perfumes to disguise the smell of vomit and purging when it was all over. I would also start eating my stocks on the way home, cramming food into my mouth, vomiting and purging into a gutter, or if I could make it, behind a bush or in an alley-way, if necessary. I'd buy more goodies, too, on the way home, just in case I ran out by the time I reached my flat, where I would quickly lock the door, take the phone off the hook and draw the curtains, get the washing-up bowl from the kitchen and put it on the living-room floor alongside all the food. Then I would kneel down in front of both (on many occasions still not having removed my coat or jacket), and eat, vomit, eat, vomit, eat, vomit, until exhausted. Sometimes however, exhaustion didn't set in immediately; I needed more! So I'd rush out again to get some more food, and come back to the gruesome scene:

Stuff, sick, stuff,
Sick, stuff, stuff.
Help me please, SOME-ONE
–there's just not enough.

Oh God! now I stink,
Empty bowl into loo,
Get rid of smell – HELP
– someone. Who am I? – WHO?

(November 1986)

38

The whole scenario would then be rounded off with those 200 laxatives. All a part of the terrifying routine, which was further compounded by confrontations with some chemists who had obviously begun to notice my rather frequent visits to their pharmacy or shop. On my road map of Brighton and Hove I had marked fifty places where I could purchase my purgatives but, even so, I was becoming a regular to them all. It was, too, quite difficult – despite meticulous efforts on my part – to be sure I rotated my visits to each.

Just like my anorexia, this was all very, very secretive, and the speed with which my bulimia developed was incredible. As with anorexia, despite being the opposite end of the spectrum, bulimia was still a coping mechanism for emotions, centred around food and self-punishment and it had the same devastating effects. It ruined any social life. Overeating made me feel too depressed, and disgusted and ashamed, and by now my body was having difficulty keeping down all the laxatives, too. After seventeen years of them, they suddenly began to make me feel nauseous as well as giving me immense pain. Worse still was to come, – despite the quantity, they didn't always have the desired effect, and on those occasions I would make hot water bottles to hold against my tummy to encourage the things to work. Sometimes they did, sometimes they didn't. Always they left burn marks on my skin as I held them against bare flesh in a fervent attempt to make them do something.

I had discovered that purgatives worked best administered with hot liquid, and so now I was trying warmth from the outside as well as the inside, with the use of the hot water bottles. Baths were out. One, they were too painful – my bones bruised so easily – but two, I felt too disgusted with, and by, myself, and didn't want to see my revolting body. After 1985 baths were a non-event and in that repulsion of myself, hair-washing I only did when it was desperately in need of washing, and I would/could no longer look in a mirror – to comb my hair, to apply make-up, etc. I just went to work hoping my appearance was passable. I used strong smelling scent too – I hated myself so much by now and changed my clothes and underwear as infrequently as possible, despite the probability that the latter might be soiled from incontinence and involuntary bowel movements. I felt absolutely worthless and bulimia nervosa, more than anorexia nervosa, I think, compounded my low self-esteem.

Eating when bingeing was never slow, it was always fast and furious. I can see now, and at times even then, that it was partly a means of expressing my frustration. Also my anger – but anger was something to which I never could or would admit. Me angry? Why? Impossible! I was too frail and small to be angry, and anyway, having been on the receiving end of so much anger I didn't like it. But eating like I did – stuffing it all down today, as if there were no tomorrow (and perhaps there might not be!), was quite an angry gesture. I was stuffing my anger and emotions back down some days, starving them away on others and always being sure of the two back-up procedures, ie, vomiting and purging those emotions up and out. I WAS NOT GOING TO FEEL ANYTHING, just as I was not going to weigh more than four stones. I continued to remain at this weight, thus avoiding the dreaded weight gain, but out of this whole horrid process my guilt, shame, self-repugnance and disgust deepened, as did my depression and self-deprecation, whilst self-esteem, self-worth and self-respect plummeted. I had no confidence at all. All I did have was a profoundly low opinion of myself.

In some ways my bulimic side was worse than the anorexia. By becoming thin, I was certainly giving out a message, albeit the symptom of 'extreme dieting/slimming', but bingeing and bulimia was something no-one knew about and since I was not putting on weight with it people were none the wiser. I was, though. I knew what I was doing. And I was terrified. Life was oppressive, paralysing chaos. Laxatives, diuretics and suppositories were costing upwards of £45 per week; money spent on food was on average £50 a day. Laundry bills were £10 weekly at least, and the amount spent on air fresheners and colognes, and the like, must have been at least £20 weekly. Hence my eating disorder, besides costing me my life, was costing me a lot of money. About

£425 each week. Despite the shoplifting, debts started to loom on the horizon, and I had to dip into all my savings.

I knew I was wasting my life as well as my money, which rapidly started to run out. I just could not die and I managed to continue existing lost now in my compulsive behaviour which enabled me to kid myself further. I wasn't really ill, my behaviour had somehow become a habit, nothing more. It had become impossible, as I think it invariably does with anyone suffering an eating disorder, to decipher whether there was a trigger to my behaviour or compulsion alone ruled. Whatever, to look on it simply as a habit was the next safety-valve. After all, habits can be given up fairly easily!

In the midsummer of 1985 I was eventually caught shop-lifting, and in fact, because nothing deterred me, was sub-sequently arrested three times. On each occasion I was escorted to the police station and locked in a cell before making a statement. Finger print taking and identification photos followed. Fortunately for me, now, (I didn't think so at the time), I received a caution after each offence and I thank, with all my heart, the policeman who arrested me that third time. He noticed the contents of my spree – a little food and 800 laxatives. He confronted me with my problem, which I firmly denied of course, and told me that my caution was conditional. I was advised to seek psychiatric treatment, alternatively the case would be brought to court. I was also warned that if caught again I would have to go to court, under medical supervision or otherwise. I hated that police officer – although I'm very grateful to him now – he knew I was ill. (I learned recently, when I went back to that police station, recovered and well, to thank them for their compas-sion and insight, that the police officer himself had been the father of an anorectic daughter. Unfortunately, due to promotion, he had moved areas so I was unable to speak to him personally. I only hope that he and his daughter are now experiencing or will experience life without an eating disorder).

As a consequence of being discovered a thief, and as someone who had anorexia, my hatred of everything grew all the stronger. I didn't care – even when sitting in those prison cells, I couldn't feel any more self-degraded. Even one particular arrest where I was behind bars for many hours (there had, I understand, been a serious outbreak of fighting football supporters which had called all 'hands to the pump'), nothing mattered any more.

A few weeks earlier, on 21st December, I had been brutally raped by two men on my way home from work. They had threatened me with a knife, and being scared beyond words I obeyed their commands and went into the park near my flat, where both men indulged in violent physical and oral rape. I'd hated myself too much to report it. I just wasn't worth it. I deserved to be put in prison, and when sent home, out of the police prison cell, I experienced once again my own self-imprisonment, and the prison I now felt my flat to be. I turned to my diary to try and express it all, and sitting on the settee at 7.00 p.m. on that bitter wintry Saturday evening, shivering with cold and shock wrote the following entry. I didn't bother with any heat or comforts in the flat. I wasn't worth it.

> *Looking at people through real bars now,*
> *I want this a reality – but how?*
> *Tonight I sat in a cold, dreary, damp empty cell,*
> *And it really wasn't anything like my hell.*
> *Not the one where I'm locked in this awful room*
> *Silent, supposedly safe in a secret cocoon.*
> *Everyone saw me, but no-one could tell*
> *How cold and how empty I feel in* my *cell.*
> *I'm tired of just waiting, wondering how long will*
>   *it be,*
> *Praying and hoping someone has the key.*
> *The key to my prison,*
> *The key to my cell.*
> *I'm certain there isn't one now – I can tell.*
> *All I want, God, is not this flat, nor my cell*
> *I want to go to prison or be punished in hell.*
> *I don't long to escape, I don't want now to be free,*

42

Nor be part of the world and life that I see.
But oh! what will happen when my sentence is
  served,
– and I come back, here, still unheard?
Oh Lord please, listen, I just really must die.
Why don't you let me? Why, why, why?
Those people I watch, spying on them all,
Talk of life being fun, being one great ball.
Please give all your great love to them
– I don't need it – life's mayhem.
I'd like now, to close all the doors, die tonight,
– please, God, let me do so – sleep forever, sleep
  tight.

The anorexia which had initially served as such a good escape and a good way of hiding, had dove-tailed. I now felt imprisoned by it. It was no longer a 'safe and secret cocoon'. I was trapped by both the frying pan and the fire! And the devil I knew as well as the devil I didn't! That night I took a mass overdose of medication and woke up the next morning in hospital. Further action involved being sectioned, and the wheel of doctors and psychiatric therapy started, running from 1986 to 1989 – and my eating disorder worsened, as I went into therapy and into limbo.

INTO THERAPY, INTO LIMBO

Although psychiatric therapy was something about which I had no choice if the police were not going to prosecute, I immediately saw it as, or rather expected it to be, the cure. I would be better soon! But it was not to be, and during the last few years of my eating disorder I felt more despairing, more hurt, more helpless, more suicidal, and hell-bent on killing myself to get away from the world. A world I hated and resented and where nobody understood, not even the 'professionals', as I was to discover.

Just as in most areas, there was very little outside support in Sussex and some of the medics I saw within the psychiatric services were against support groups; they appeared to view the disorder as physical, therefore demanding the so-simple process of eating. The problem of lack of expertise in anorexia and bulimia nervosa was a really chronic one, and with varying viewpoints and attitudes from different medics, I felt in a real chaos and a 'wierdo'.

I remember one doctor, having seen me twice weekly as an out-patient for two years (which followed a period of being sectioned into hospital several times, and on other occasions, although I think this was to escape from the world and food, being admitted as a voluntary patient, discharging myself after a few days refuge), saying that he just could not relate to me. Perhaps he was voicing his own despair and frustration, but he chose the analogy of an alcoholic, towards whom he could identify. As a person who enjoyed drinking socially himself, he could understand the 'good feeling' and lack of tension and worries that one experiences to some degree in enjoying a little drink and how it might be possible to abuse this method of semi-oblivion by adopting it as a mechanism for blotting out on a full-time scale. However, someone with my problem was totally incomprehensible. Food tasted nice, it was essential for keeping going, ie, living, and eating was a pleasurable and sometimes a social experience, which often picked one up, if tired, for example. Lack of food made one ill.

'You have something, and are doing something', he said, 'which I just don't understand'.

I can remember at that point wondering whether to shout at him, scream, cry, or run out of the room. Instead silence ruled and I gave way to quiet desperation and an awful envy of alcoholics. I just wished alcohol was my problem. At least people seemed to recognise, respect and understand it, and anyway all the alcoholic had to do was give up the drink! I couldn't give up my habit – food, or starvation. I'd have to go on eating forever. The thought alarmed me. Go on like this? Eat – never – I couldn't.

After that particular session, I ran out to my car, bought a portion of six fishcakes and chips in each of the ten fish and chip shops within the vicinity of my home, along with as many laxatives as I could steal from a self-service drug store, and 200 Paracetamol. I got home, gorged on the whole smelly, salty, vinegary, soggy mess and swallowed the tablets. Then I waited... I don't know how long I waited – according to my television video-clock I woke up two days later – on the kitchen floor. I'd obviously defaecated and urinated in that coma. I was filthy. The kitchen was filthy. We both stank. My only salvation in all that was getting on to the weighing scales with immediate terror, because I was sure I hadn't vomited back/up all those calories, to find that I'd lost almost half a stone. (Dehydration.) As a 'reward' for my weight loss, I felt confident enough to refind my control again to starve – and I did – for another few weeks. I felt in control again.

Every time I visited a psychiatric hospital, whether for out-patient treatment or to be admitted as an in-patient, I always sensed what I described as an aura of enmity towards me from the nursing staff. It almost seemed as if a violent, or suicidal person, manic depressive, or schizophrenic was welcome. I, who at least behaved fairly well in the waiting room or recovery room, and was of reasonable appearance and had an obvious degree of intelligence was not! Again I felt the odd one out! The same feeling that had permeated most of my life. However, I do know that this 'enmity' was not totally of my imagination. One particular nurse, Julia, of whom I became rather fond, and she of me, I believe, because she always found time to try and listen to me, as well as explain quite honestly her lack of understanding of eating disorders, confessed that most of the psychiatric staff did indeed dread treating anorectic patients. It was always a battle, forcing food down them, and then having to watch their every move, checking mattresses and other possible hiding places for uneaten food or vomit. To me this enhanced even further the total lack of compassion. Staff and doctors and psychiatrists sometimes appeared as ogres, and fierce, or tough but reasonably compassionate. The latter seemed to be willing to share my pain, but they used only the stick and never the carrot to compel me to eat. On top of that, hospital food was real junk food – stodgy, sickly, fatty, greasy, unhealthy and was hardly served up in an appealing way. To me this mattered very much. Perhaps to the schizophrenic or manic depressive it doesn't; they gobbled it up and shovelled it in without worry. To me it was torment to eat such stuff. And surely, hardly nutritious for developing a well body and mind? (A consideration that was greatly respected in my last hospital admission, into an eating disorder specialist clinic.)

During these years, therapy was a hocus-pocus – on both sides. I was conjuring up deception on my side, and I felt they were on theirs. Treatments as in-patient were various, as they tried to fatten me up (as I saw it), or make me better (as they seemed to see it). There was the reward and punishment system, the dangling the carrot system, and 'go along with her' system. They also tried a little psychology therapy.

The first form of treatment happened by accident. I had agreed to be admitted, voluntarily, into a psychiatric unit, and quite what expectations were on both sides I haven't a clue. I suppose I had hoped, as I did every now and then, that I would be cured. I just remember my first meal, breakfast (I had been admitted the previous evening, very late). It consisted of fruit juice, porridge, a pint of milk, coffee, bacon, fried eggs, two sausages and tomato, and four slices of buttered white bread with jam. I freaked! Refused all food for a week and lost over one and a half stones! The nursing staff then decided to take things away from me if I didn't eat. But I didn't care – I hadn't come with many personal possessions, nor had I come with much self esteem/respect; I was really past caring about myself. When I was down to just my nightie, and all treats (such as watching TV, or having a bath), having, at the same time, been forbidden, I was put in a single locked room, with just a commode and a bed, covered with one sheet. My nightie was taken away from me – along with any nth of self-pride I might just have managed to hold on to – and I was told I could regain it, and other desired possessions, when I ate. I started eating again – but only just enough to merit the reward, and only enough to get back an acceptable amount of clothing in which to abscond. 'Dressed', I smashed the commode into the window, climbed out, and ran out of the grounds, and actually hitched an immediate lift to Eastbourne. There, purchasing several packets of Anadin, I went to the Ladies on the train station and took the lot. The police, having been alerted about my 'runner', found me. I was taken to Accident and Emergency to be stomach pumped. A spell in ITU followed and I was sectioned back to the psychiatric hospital. There they greeted me with the news 'We are going to try and work with you', – I was offered as many laxatives as I wanted, when I felt I needed them!! I couldn't believe it. Again the desperation was immense and I guessed they too were at the point of not knowing quite what to do, except try and keep me alive. My disbelief, however, was justified – when I asked for my usual 200 Sennakot, the doctor explained that they were only allowed to give a maximum of two to each person, daily, and that they hadn't the stocks or funds to support my needs, despite their promise to 'work with me'. I thus altered my line of attack in what was appearing to be a battle. I 'served' my section, appearing to be a willing patient, eating (albeit only very small amounts), and presenting a reasonably pleasant personality, but with only one goal in mind – to get out, and be four stones again.

I thus ate my way out of hospital as I did on many occasions, and they had fattened me up. It was always the same; they got my weight up and I would then get it back down. I went straight down to four stones each time I returned home (by very foul, rather than fair, means). They had fed me up, and I was fed up, literally, with their attitude. They fed me up and fattened me up, which resulted in me feeling fed-up and fat, and fed-up ready to destroy it all; I was also left feeling very depressed.

It was a long long time before treatment offered any sort of counselling. Instead my psychiatrist kept trying to pinpoint something, maybe traumas in my childhood. Nothing surfaced and I was briefly transferred to a psychologist. In these particular sessions again I wasn't sure quite what was the objective. As I understood it, a psychologist was someone who would re-educate my behavioural patterns, at the same time trying to analyse my mental state, whilst a psychiatrist's role was that of studying and treating mental disorders. Anyway, I did not spend long in psychology – the psychologist was very keen to talk about sex and sexual matters. He concluded that as a child I had not masturbated enough and suggested that the next session should be a bath, in his presence, when he would instruct me in masturbation! Needless to say I was quite put off this sort of help, and, in fact, so confused, I just went home vowing never to have a bath again, ever, and never ever touch myself anywhere. In all fairness to that gentleman, though, perhaps he had struck on something, but not I felt, or feel to be the answer. As a child I remember being told that anything to do with your bottom was rude; perhaps, then, I had never sought the comfort a child can get from masturbation on a healthy level. Thus my utter repugnance and horror and disgust, as well as embarrassment, at his suggestion.

Having gone from pillar to post, I then went back to the pillar – to psychiatry, this time undergoing sessions (I don't call it counselling, because counselling I consider to be working with a person, offering them guidance towards developing a well being), to try and find the cause of my eating disorder. It seemed and was – and is, I feel, dangerous to concentrate solely on cause and effect. I couldn't unearth any one particular trauma or circumstance, and anything I did mention as being distressful was always something for more deep and meaningful discussion. I felt at the time there was the possibility of making mountains out of molehills and I also felt greater despair. Everytime we had one of these 'deep and meaningful' discussions it seemed as if there was pressure on me to be well afterwards. We had struck gold! I should be OK now I had got this off my chest, but I wasn't. I was made to feel even more of a peculiarity because I couldn't, or at one point as my psychiatrist suggested, wouldn't, talk about the cause. The thing was I didn't know the cause, and in fact, I thought then, as I firmly believe now, there wasn't one. Blame cannot be apportioned to any one thing or person; it is a culmination of many things, events and emotions, although of course, there may be a catalyst that actually finally tips the boat. I also feel that had I, for example, been able to say I was raped at eleven and developed an eating disorder, it could have provided my anorexia/bulimia nervosa with an excuse to carry on, ie, 'I was raped at eleven, therefore I have every right to have an eating disorder and behave as I do'. And a focal point on which a psychiatrist could solely concentrate.

Weighing me at every session was not something that was continued, and my psychiatrist was loath to talk about food. Good or bad I don't know. With regard to being weighed it was a pretty useless affair. Every time before I went to the doctor, I would water-load twenty five cups of water (which represents 11 lb), and wear weights in my clothing. As a PE teacher, I had learned, on a basic level, the art of snorkling, which demanded wearing a weighted belt, and I used those weights (4 lb each), for my weigh-ins. Oddly enough I was always weighed clothed, so I was laughing, or was I? Being deceitful was handed me on a plate and I took it, but it got me nowhere. Further, I was tying the doctors' hands behind their backs – crying out for help, but doing practically everything against their wishes, ie, being honest. And, of course, too, I was being dishonest to myself – continuing to kid myself that I would be OK soon, I could cope. Meanwhile, I was providing myself with more ammunition for hating myself – I was being so deceitful. More room for self-hatred and self-loathing, and no room for self-respect. I viewed medical help as punitive, so it was obvious, in retrospect, that I would never get well.

As time went on, except for the conditions placed on me regarding receiving psychiatric help, I never really understood the point of it. Tuesday appointments, five o'clock every week, were just duty visits, which towards the end I sometimes cancelled (because by then the chronicity of my self-abuse was finally taking its toll and I felt too weak. I suppose I was actually dying – but not as I had hoped – quickly, instead very slowly and agonisingly). The medics had given me a label – 'anorectic', ie, a problem with body concepts and food, and I accepted the label, because, manipulative as I was, I turned it to my convenience. I felt that I was doing it all to myself, that, for the majority of the time, anyway, I was in control and that since we couldn't unearth any reasons for it, it did not qualify as a proper illness. Obviously I was just a little bit off my trolley! I believed, quite sincerely, that I would be able to turn off all the emotions that I had so carefully sensitised, whenever I wanted to. However, one thing I did gain from my therapy was the realisation that I had so rigorously organised my behaviour to the extent that I found it impossible to stop when I wanted to. This, though, as I mentioned in the previous chapter, I interpreted as just a habit. A bit like smoking – something which could be stopped, but which might be a weeny bit difficult occasionally! And there was always tomorrow! My mind always seemed to talk to me in a very logical way. I suppose it was rather like when you've had too much to drink yet are convinced your judgement is fine, so driving is no problem. Without food my thought patterns had to be askew and totally illogical (after all if my body was ill-nourished, so, too, was my brain), yet to me I was making such sense! One example I well remember is justifying yet another shop-lifting spree. This one was fine. It wasn't really stealing because I didn't intend using or doing anything with the stuff!

One very positive thing that came from these years of medical treatment, albeit for only a short time, was that I suddenly began to yearn for tomorrow, a real tomorrow, when I really would stop being ill, and be well, instead of dreaming about a tomorrow that I knew would never come, because of the reality of recovery being a very painful and long time. I began to want to leave my eating disorder behind me and not die, but my anorexia/bulimia, having the upper hand, told me it was too late. Psychiatric therapy had resulted in nothing, had unearthed nothing and was becoming terrifying. I couldn't talk about my feelings because except for the fear of being fat, I didn't know what they were, and any attempts I made to express them resulted in me being made to feel ridiculed. I hadn't cried for twenty years, and was scared of doing so in case of never being able to stop. (Rather like my fears behind stopping vomiting and purging, and eating properly – I was sure that once I started eating proper amounts of food, I would never be able to stop.) All I could do was starve, binge, purge, vomit. I'd starve before my weekly session, and spend that hour thinking of the gorge to follow. What I would get, and from which shops. Binges were now constituting as much as 10,000 calories a day, and the amount of purgatives was doubling. I was still keeping my weight in the four stone bracket, but my stomach and bowels were distended and I had to hide them under baggy clothing.

Now I had no choice; I really had something to cover up, not fat, but distension from gross malnutrition and laxative-abuse. My skin had become very, very dry, splitting and cracking, and unable to heal, particularly the sides of my mouth, which were constantly bleeding too. My stomach lining ruptured and I lost the lining to my bowel, developing severe haemorrhoids. My eyes became bloodshot, my throat often bled, and I had awful mouth ulcers, all as a result of the continued vomiting and purging. My face and throat also took on a puffiness, which I could only get rid of by more purging, and thus dehydration. However, I still carried on, feeling myself to be in limbo, wondering whether I was on the borders of hell, just waiting to drop into the fiery furnace, or just in a state of neglect, self-neglect and neglect by others. In that oblivion I readily accepted the various medications I was prescribed (and what a cocktail – treating all the intrinsic symptoms – depression, sleeplessness and tiredness and lethargy!), on many occasions altering the prescriptions, so I could take sufficient to get by on the haze that too many drugs produce. I was making a pig's ear of living, a hopeless job of killing myself, despite the repeated very serious attempts which were now more frequent, so if I had to go on living, maybe this would be the way. If I drugged myself up sufficiently, perhaps I would stop thinking about food, too, and stop being like this.

'Perhaps', however, was not to be. The haze was short-lived. I had become such a sinister, evil, person inside, nothing could or would destroy me. I turned to a Christian Science healer at one point, and on another occasion actually went through a bona-fide exorcism ritual at a church, because it was considered possible that I might be possessed. I *felt* possessed, and the self-hatred was enormous – an all-consuming giant. I did not realise that everything had to come from me if I was to recover; I blithely thought I could ask for the (magical) cure from someone else.

In 1988 I swung back to wanting to be rid of anorexia/bulimia by dying; I was sure of my decision, I had been dancing on my grave long enough now, it was time to stop the dance and get into my coffin:

Oh! earth beneath my feet
Let me be under you.
Oh! wooden box to be my coffin
Let me be in you.

I don't want a funeral,
I don't want anyone to know.
All I do want
– is to be allowed to go.

I'm a devil, not a person.
No-one need, or will, cry for me.
No-one cares and I don't
Oh Ann! There's no more time for tea.

Hate, more than ever, surrounded everything: I hated me, hated the way I looked, hated the now apparent total lack of control over eating, which, when I did have it in the beginning, I had scurrilously enjoyed (enhanced, no doubt, by the initial compliments of approval as I lost weight), and I hated the way everyone saw me; or rather, in retrospect, the way I thought people saw me. I had tried, in therapy, and, to a degree, elsewhere, running from one person to another – getting superficial love and support and sympathy, until it became too claustrophobic and intrusive, and food became the issue once more. Then I would run on.

The same with my work; I kept on seeking promotion. One, I couldn't stop demanding better and better performance levels from myself, and two, I couldn't stay for long in one place, in case people got to know me too well – they might suss me out, and I was hopeless at socialising. I couldn't put down roots professionally or personally. I was trying to run away from myself in the end, and actually started to run back and forth to the hospital as a voluntary patient. I felt I couldn't trust myself. In an effort to avoid food and shops, I chose the scenic, more often longest route to and from work. But once there (work or home), I'd pick up the phone and order take-away after take-away.

Feeling that this might be noticed by colleagues and neighbours, I then started going out to restaurants instead, ordering great quantities of lavish foods, vomiting between each course and going on from one restaurant to another. On those occasions, I can remember telling myself that I had to taste every food possible in main courses and sweets, and thus presented myself with a task and challenge that *had* to be met. Hence many a night I would visit half a dozen places in order to taste pasta, meat, fish, eggs, and cheese, creamy sweet gooey gâteaux, chocolate, steam puddings and custard, trifle and ice cream. One evening, between 6.00 p.m. and 1.00 a.m., I had visited, and binged in nine restaurants, going home twice in between in order to change food and vomit-stained clothing. Further, having rather embarrassingly, in the sixth restaurant discovered I had run out of cheques I did a runner to avoid the confrontation with the bill. It scared me, but not enough. I vomited in a gutter in a backstreet, by my doctor's surgery (which unfortunately was adjacent to a road full of eating places), and did the very same thing in restaurants seven, eight and nine. I couldn't stop. I almost felt possessed, and occasionally felt most certainly so.

I think despair was a feeling shared on all sides in this hocus-pocus, and although I think it a great shame that the medics couldn't understand, I do not blame them. Possibly, even though *I* thought I was, they could see that I was *not* willing to try to live my life without my eating disorder. Paradoxically it seemed to be the only identification I had, anorexia/bulimia. All they could do, it seemed, as a next stage was to tolerate it. They allowed me to run in and out of help, by giving me 'open house' to the psychiatric unit in Brighton, to be admitted when I wanted to, even if for the wrong reasons, ie, not to work towards recovery, rather to escape from food, the world, from my routines, my stealing, my bingeing and purging. They even endured short three-day spells, despite my refusing to eat. Perhaps they felt helpless – my doing perhaps, because I never felt I 'got on with anyone' when food became the issue, but nevertheless I guess they felt that they had a duty to keep me alive. Thus, towards the end, my Tuesday sessions took on the role of probationer, I reported I was alive. Likewise on Thursday mornings, it was arranged that a community psychiatric nurse should visit me, to talk, if I wished, and give me a Depoxil injection (a form of anti-depressant and tranquilliser that helps people to keep on an even keel). Eileen got to know my bottom very well – more perhaps than my face! She always stayed for the apportioned hour, her on the settee, me hunched up over a hot water bottle, on my bean-bag, sideways to her, and we exchanged very few words. It might have been during the summer heatwaves, when everyone was sunbathing and the sky was blue, but to me the day was dark, grey and cold.

Gradually I became too ill to work, and for the first time in my life had a poor record of attendance. I suppose I had managed to stay in work despite my appearance, because my work output was of a very good standard, and likewise my attendance. I had very few days off sick. Now though, I was having too many sick days, and this in a new job, as community charge inspector for Brighton Borough Council. Taking laxatives was becoming inordinately difficult. They seemed to make me gag. I split the 200 into two one hundreds, and would set my alarm clock to take the first dose at 3.30 a.m. and the second at 7.00 a.m. Not that I was sleeping, but I did nod occasionally. At 3.30 a.m. and 7.00 a.m., I would make a boiling hot mug of black coffee in the kitchen and try and swallow each hundred, as appropriate, shoving the tablets in in fistfuls, but sometimes I couldn't control the retching effect they had on me and would bring them back up in the sink. Desperate, I can remember spooning up what I had brought up, determined to successfully administer the correct dosage, but occasionally I lost the battle. I then had to break the 'fix' down into four lots of fifty. At the same time, though, because as earlier mentioned the laxatives didn't appear to always produce results, this whole scenario scared me. I was frightened that I wouldn't be able to eat at all now if I couldn't purge – I'd have to regain that wonderful starvation control, but I knew deep down that this was impossible, the more so if I was going to put myself under pressure

55

to do this. I really felt as if I was just existing. I couldn't focus or concentrate on television, I lost all interest in my hobbies and I lay in bed most of the day, curtains drawn, often not able to get to the toilet in time to be sick or open my bowels. Whatever the weather and temperature, I kept those curtains drawn. I preferred the darkness, and the bed was piled high with blankets despite my electric blanket being on high. To keep some sanity, I suppose, I kept the radio on, very low, but hated all the presenters when they greeted their listeners with bright good news and cheery hallos. It meant another day had dawned and I was still alive.

It all seemed more poignant the onset of Christmas of 1989. Everyone was happy out there, Christmas was coming, we should be merry. Not me, though, my cupboards were bare, as were they always at Christmas, full only of 3000 laxatives, 100 suppositories and 500 Paracetamol to get through the twelve days of Christmas. Not forgetting to also mention the 300 diuretics.

I was now becoming unreliable at both my full-time job, and in my part-time bar work. Often I would phone up last minute, saying I was unable to come in, so of course was letting people down and getting myself a poor reputation. I was no longer able to put on an act, my work was punctuated with errors, things I had forgotten to do, and mistakes I had made. I wasn't able to keep up my excellent standards, and the respect that people had had for me in this field began to wain. I knew I was failing, knew I was dying and the longing to die, now an obsessive dream, became a fear. Scott Fitzgerald wrote, 'The fear of death can become a longing for death.' I identified with it one hundred percent. I longed for death now because I feared it; I now reckoned it could be a fearful process, not a kind, gentle release as I had at first thought. My faith, which was enough to quickly send up desperate prayers every now and then to Someone whom I referred to as God, allowed me to consider what life after death might mean. Everyone speaks of the tranquillity in the life hereafter, but in having turned to biblical passages, guided by the Christian Science healer, it was plausible to me that if I didn't make my peace here, before I died, then death – an eternal life – would only be a dreadful hell, and forever I would never be at rest.

It was one day when lying in bed, barely able to move or breathe, I pondered on the above subject and on all my fears. In sheer terror I telephoned a friend, Pammy, who had the spare key to my flat. She let herself in and persuaded me to call the doctor. I did, I don't know why, I knew he couldn't do anything, but I suppose I just hoped. The doctor visited about 8.00 p.m. On sight he immediately thought I was yet again sectionable (I gathered later that he didn't think I would last the night – and boy! did I hate him for not letting me die), and a psychiatrist and social worker were called to the flat to assess the situation. I vividly recall trying to defend my case against hospitalisation. I was OK and poured out all the reasons for being OK, even getting up and showing them I was capable of moving. I denied their suggestion that I was very ill and had answers for everything they said, except one. The social worker asked me why, if I was well, did I have eight blankets on my bed, the electric blanket on high, along with a hot water bottle in the bed, and socks and a jumper on over the top of my nightie, when we were currently in the midst of a heatwave, and the outside temperature, even at that time of night (about 11.00 p.m.), was in the latter eighties. I was stumped. And I was sectioned.

This admission was my last one before seeking specialist help, and oh, was I angry! I even hit out at the ambulance-men when they came to collect me and struggled continuously all the way to hospital, resorting to biting the men when it was obvious I could not match their strength. I decided to appeal against my section, which was a twenty eight-day one, and the appeal came up on the nineteenth day. By then I had obviously gained weight, having had drips, intravenous feeding and then food, and I had summoned the help of a solicitor. Together we appeared before a jury consisting of an independent psychiatrist, a

57

doctor and a layman, us on one side, my psychiatrist, who was all for sectioning me a further six months, on the other. I was bright and chirpy on the surface, obviously made a good case for myself and we won, despite me weighing in at just over five stones. I blew my psychiatrist a raspberry, felt ecstatic and walked out free, or rather walked out of the hospital. When I arrived home, the cold loneliness hit immediately. It was not freedom. I got into the car to go steal all the purgatives I could lay my hands on, to get my weight back down to four stones, but when they hadn't worked by 5.30 that evening, I went out to the late night chemist, bought 200 Paracetamol and overdosed. Again I survived this brutal attack, waking up several days later, on the kitchen floor, and suffering no liver damage either. This time, however, it was the end. I went straight back to the psychiatric unit, as a voluntary patient to be admitted. Only, though, as far as I was concerned, for a few days refuge. Or maybe a week, or more if I could stick it.

It was during this ten-day spell that I encountered an eating disorder therapist, for the first time. I was told he was prepared to counsel me, if I ate. I readily agreed, because I was now thinking along the lines of, 'Well if you're fat, but happy, never mind'. I was dismayed to be greeted solely with the words, 'Use me', I asked him how, I asked him all sorts of questions, but he just kept saying, 'Use me'. I felt useless and incompetent, and was absolutely sure now that there was no possibility of recovering. How the hell do you use someone? Not without help of a very special kind, which was the one thing this therapist did let slip. There were specialist doctors and clinics, so I learned, whose entire work, centred around eating disorders, involving eating and therapy together: cognitive therapy, ie, looking at the inside (whilst also treating the outside). I demanded to be placed on the application list for assessment. At first my psychiatrist refused – he thought my case to be too chronic and serious, and quite blatantly told me I would be turned down at the assessment, if I indeed got that far. I demanded my rights, knowing that I was allowed to request a second opinion, and reluctantly my psychiatrist agreed. He wrote a letter on my behalf to a specialist clinic, and, to his amazement, I was accepted for interview, and shortly afterwards, placement. I immediately decided to discharge myself from the Brighton unit at this point, go home and wait, and just let things get worse. I was also intent on starving myself completely. This would be my last chance and I had to be thin enough and unwell enough to be treated! So ran my (totally illogical) thought patterns. I told myself that however bad this interim period was going to be, never mind, I'd soon be better, now; there was light at the end of the tunnel, I'd manage, but I had better make sure I was as thin as possible, otherwise they might turn me away for being too fat!

As it was, I did manage, but only just. I felt both grateful and relieved to receive a placement so quickly in the specialist clinic where waiting lists were, and are, so long, and applications and placements often refused. But I didn't realise that, yet again, I wasn't being honest with myself. I saw this, too, as a refuge. Somehow, despite complete bed rest and 3,000 calories a day, to reach a target weight of just over nine stones, I reckoned I'd still be thin if I made myself think thin!

I did not accept my placement because I wanted to be free of my eating disorder, rather because I was frightened of living, and just couldn't die. Goodness knows what the specialists saw in me on interview for that placement. I have since learned that they can only afford to accept patients who have a positive attitude towards recovery, and in whom they see that potential. I must have lied so well, and come over so well. I know I didn't dare tell them the truth, dare tell them just how many purgatives, etc, I was taking, nor for how many years, nor how much food I was bingeing. I was scared of being thought too hopeless a case, as my psychiatrist had intimated, and a lost cause. I was scared of not being accepted.

I cannot remember much about the interview at all, nor what I said, any more than what was said to me. So the next stage, the road to recovery, was a very long hard one, the more so because of this. I came to realise just what it did mean with a jolt, once I had been admitted, and I felt as if I had been dropped onto the road, like one is thrown in at the deep end of the swimming pool in order to learn to swim immediately. My options were plain; I could go forwards, towards the road to recovery, or be discharged. I chose to go forward. I was too scared of the outside world, and perhaps that was just as well because the road to recovery, although a long, hard, bumpy, agonisingly painful one, was certainly worth travelling.

MY ROAD TO RECOVERY

The fact that I am free now is only because I eventually ACCEPTED that it was me who had the power to do anything about recovering from my eating disorder. And it was me who had to make the choice. Sure, I'd been told this before – that it had to come from me, and I suppose that I'd half realised it, but the key was that I had not accepted it. Live or die – eventually, no-one could 'make me better'. Of course the length and severity of my illness involved a very long period of hospitalisation to start out on the road to recovery, starting being the operative word. I was not discharged 'better' or 'cured', simply my journey towards a full recovery had begun. Again I had thought differently; that this admission to the clinic would be it – I'd go back into the community well, with everything behind me. Although I was to find out just how mistaken I was, I'm sure that thinking as I did, even be it once again kidding myself, helped me hang on and stay the course. A course which was very rough and extremely turbulent, and which HURT. I remember telling myself, 'OK, you've got to put on five stones (target weight now being nine stones two pounds). You won't like it at first, you'll be fat, but so what if you're better? You'll get used to it.' It was with these thoughts I entered the specialist clinic for eating disorders, in London.

The one main difference between this last admission and the others was that here I had volunteered to go in, and actually signed a contract, as a sort of agreement to abide by the clinic's disciplines. However, within a few weeks I was once again reconsidering the whole thing. I began to see putting

61

on the weight as something *THEY* were making me do; *THEY* were making me fat, I had not signed a contract to become fat.

The first few days of my admission were almost bliss – I was allowed to eat (being given my food and fluids at regular intervals), and it seemed as if my void and emptiness were being filled up – with food. In fact, I felt so much better and relieved, I actually began to think once again that I didn't really have any emotional problems. My difficulties lay quite simply in 'the pursuit of thinness'. After four or five days, though, showing a terrific weight gain of twelve pounds (as my body absorbed both the 3,000 daily calorie allowance and re-hydrated), I also began to *FEEL*, and anything other than bliss. I felt fat, frightened, miserable and resentful. Nobody had explained that the great and inevitable initial weight gain was usual because the body was absorbing all the fluid it could. I thought I had gained twelve pounds of body tissue, ie, fat, and had visions that before long I would be a Michelin Tyre man, unable to stop gaining weight, unless I stopped eating again, and a contender for the dance group 'The Roly-Polys' (an audition which I would be sure to fail because I was too fat!). I LONGED to be thin again, and hated myself for volunteering to be admitted.

Of course, as a voluntary patient, I was also free to discharge myself, and although I did attempt to do this on a couple of occasions (without success; a section was threatened because I was so suicidal), I was too scared of going back into the community, too scared of the eating disorder hell. The hospital represented a haven from all that, yet at the same time I felt as if I was between the devil and the deep blue sea. Thin or fat, it was no different. Eating and gaining weight were not making me feel better, but making me feel worse!

Exactly what weight gain was supposed to do, apart from the obvious gaining of weight, was actually to make one feel worse, initially. So I was right on course, so to speak, although I didn't realise it. As one gains weight, so one regains feelings and becomes more in touch with oneself.

Hence up come a lot of feelings that might have been starved, vomited, purged or binged away. This was exactly what was happening to me. The specialist treatment was all about re-feeding and gaining weight, learning to recognise, hang on to and express feelings and emotions in a constructive way, as opposed to the destructive ways of anorexia/ bulimia nervosa, and self-analysis through cognitive therapy. I was encouraged to express my feelings on paper, in a logbook (a diary type affair), and in group meetings, involving talking, art therapy, dance and movement, assertion and relaxation instruction, and psycho-drama.

At first, and for some time, the feelings I had were of hate and resentment – of anything, everything and everyone. I knew I couldn't or shouldn't really resent the clinic or the treatment because I had volunteered to be admitted and signed the contract, so I inverted most of those angry feelings on myself. Beyond food and body-weight, shape and size, though, I didn't know why I felt so strongly, except for one other concern – visitors. I didn't want any. I didn't want them to see one, how fat I was getting (I was still at a chronically low, abnormal body-weight but my mind was not capable of thinking logically), and two, how much better I looked (especially my face as it had filled out with the re-hydrating process, and quite rapidly too). They would make comments and seemed to think I was getting better, or, at worst, intimated I *was* better or should be better. This just made me feel worse than ever. I have to admit, though, that rather like them, and the media too perhaps, I kept hoping that the recovery *would* be quite magical. I guess I just couldn't take any more pain; the mental anguish over the years had worn me down, I had forgotten the Army's motto 'No gain without pain'. There were also a few visitors much later on who came to see me after I had reached my target weight who, I suppose, having been used to seeing a very slight me, actually voiced the fact that they didn't think all this weight suited me! A very unhelpful comment that and cruel, because weight and body-tissue gain is initially very flabby, particularly when you remember that it is all gained whilst on complete bed-rest; ie, without any permitted exercising or mobilising. It does, in fact take, on average, six months to 'shift' around and disperse more evenly, some turning into muscle as the body tolerates a normal amount of exertion. However, it was hard to remember and hang on to that fact, at first, as I looked at my huge belly, bottom, hips, bust and treble chin, with excess fat even hanging down under the upper arms and making the thighs wobble enormously!

As my weight went up, so my feelings and the emotional pain became greater. I had tried all sorts of ways of bribing myself to stay, to see the treatment through. I adopted the attitude that I'd swallow all these calories like medicine, close my eyes until it was all over, convincing myself that reaching nine stones two pounds would mean I would be well again. (As silly a notion this, as had been the idea of being thin, when I thought four stones meant everything would be all right.) I kept sending up quick prayers, 'Please, God, let people like me', 'When I reach my target weight, please let me be a successful and nice person'. I was now actively reversing my former thoughts of equating thinness with success. Of course, though, I was still seeing no further than my body-weight and size; 'fat' now equalled a successful life, and 'thin' – failure.

To some degree, however, that attitude gave me hope and kept me going, but, as it and I was fantasising, I constantly experienced rude awakenings, bringing me back to reality. I would go to bed at night – always as soon as I could, after we had had the nightly cup of milk and three biscuits, to hide my new, fatter shape, and at some stage, in now managing to sleep a little (food acts like a drug; a well-fed body, and hence mind, inevitably induces better sleep), I would dream I was thin again. They were very vivid, very real dreams in which I really believed, until, along came the enemy – the morning dawn, daylight and reality. I was fat, I could never be thin again. A somewhat ironical thought, this, now, because the years I had spent at four stones I had never considered myself thin, in fact sometimes too fat! – yet here I was now, a little heavier, looking back to those 'good old (thin) days'.

A two to three pound a week weight gain was the clinic's expectation, after the initial ten days or so. How I wished it was two to three ounces! How I wished I could have more control over how much I ate, and what, and when, but all this was part of the therapy – handing over control and trust to others, who would eventually, gradually, hand it back. This was a two-way thing, of course, between the staff and me. Not only did I have to trust the staff, but they had to be able to trust me. I could lie as much as I like, swearing I'd eaten everything, not hidden anything, or thrown it out of the window, but the proof was in the scales. 'You are what you eat', was their motto. 'Yes', I thought, 'FAT'. HOW TRUE!

Depression set in very soon as I regained my feelings. It seemed as if I was physically and mentally stronger than ever and I started channelling this into complete and utter self-hatred, and the destructive thoughts returned. I wanted to die. I kept these thoughts to myself, though. I had forgotten what self-honesty was about, and as regards my logbook, I only wrote 'polite' things. This was my only control. As regards the subject on 'My Shape', for example I wrote 'Don't like it' (27th April 1990). Under 'Anxieties', one entry reads 'None' (1st May); concerning 'Sense of Self', I wrote 'Poor' (1st May), 'Triggers of my illness' – 'don't know' (13th May), 'Other Moods' – 'don't know' (16th April). My writing was small, very neat and legible. (Later, as I learned to express my feelings openly, and honestly, it became a scrawl, as my hand tried to keep up with all my thoughts as they poured out. Now, though, the anger and hatred was all under wraps, all bottled up and kept very very much under control.)

When entering the clinic, I had been advised to bring some suitable 'day-wear clothing' (ie, some clothes suitable for when I had gained weight), for attendance at group meetings. Whilst I was in the process of reaching target weight, during which time I was in a cubicle, with no company, I was only allowed to wear night clothes, and this, in fact, was the case for the entire first four weeks when no group attendance or much socialising was encouraged. (It was considered that we needed and had to have this time to use, to develop complete self-awareness.) Alongside this went complete bed rest, with a commode by the bed for when necessary, and which, because it was emptied by the nursing staff, helped to discourage the temptation to vomit. Neither were we allowed to mobilise, so our beds were made for us and wash-bowls were also brought to us, as were our meals. Regarding the clothes, I had purposely purchased some huge track-suit bottoms and a jumper (from a charity shop), as well as a couple of voluminous nighties and a dressing gown. Imagine my shock when, after that first month, I put on the tracksuit bottoms and jumper, only to find that they were too tight! I had nothing else to wear, I *had* to wear my day clothes (it was the clinic's way of helping you to gradually come to terms with your new shape and weight), and I *had* to go to, what turned out to be, the one hour art-therapy class. I forced myself out of my cubicled bed space, somehow getting there. With my head down, ashamed and embarrassed, I sat tight-lipped, through the whole class, completely de-sensitising my feelings, then RAN – all the way back. I put on my nightie again, as was expected, and refused to draw back my curtains and let the nurse bring in my lunch. Then came the tears, non-stop for half an hour, followed by an angry exchange with the said nurse who had to strictly adhere to, and enforce, the times of meals. I told her that she didn't understand, told her she hadn't a clue how to be sympathetic and despised her when she explained she couldn't alter the situation. It was the first time I had to 'go with' my feelings. I couldn't use food or laxatives, vomiting or purging, and I couldn't run away.

Looking back, that occasion was my first milestone. I had cried – for the first time in twenty years, and I had expressed some emotions, albeit somewhat harshly, and to an innocent party. At the time though, I saw it as anything but. I was gross, I was fat, there was no hope, and I used my outburst as ammunition with which to beat myself. I was really a hateful person now, being so rude! Hateful, horrid and fat!

I dreaded wearing my day clothes. I loved my big voluminous long-flowing nighties and cover-up dressing gown, and tried desperately to ignore the fact the pants I was wearing underneath were becoming too tight, too small (they were a children's size), and were leaving elastic marks on my fat fleshy thighs, bottom and tummy. I had not thought to buy any bras either – I'd only worn a bra in school for two of my teen years (and then not because I needed to but rather to be like everyone else), and I hadn't thought to expect breasts. It was horrifying when I saw what was happening, and I refused to buy any sort of bra top because I was so terrified. I couldn't face the thought of having to find out my size either. Of course, all this was greatly exaggerated in my own mind (very natural and usual; the other patients experienced similar feelings with regard to body-image), but I didn't realise that. To me it was very real. Only many months later did I see things in a better perspective and in a clearer light. Those 'huge clothes' I had purchased, prior to my admission, turned out to be size ten (I hadn't dared look when I bought them in Oxfam), and for a person almost five feet six inches, aged thirty eight, size ten represents a slim, if not too slim a figure. My body image had been hopelessly distorted, and remained so for a long time.

With my peculiar sense of optimism and belief that nine stones two pounds meant I would be better, thus ignoring my true feelings, emotions and thoughts, I *did* stay the course and got to my target weight, on Sunday evening, 3rd June 1990 at 7.10 p.m. As I stood on the weighing scales, waiting for what seemed ages for the nurse to set the bar so it gave an exact reading, I just knew I had made it. When nine stones two pounds was called out, I leapt high into the air, kissed the nurse, hugged fellow patients, ran down the corridor, laughing and shouting for joy, 'I've made it. I've done it. I'm normal'. Then, back in my bed space, the euphoria went completely. I fell straight off my 'high' into a 'low'. Another rude awakening. Reality was staring me

67

straight in the face. Here I was, nine stones two pounds. My weight was better, but *I* wasn't – I felt no different inside. I was now just a fat anorectic. I viewed what was to come (unrestricted movement on a gradual basis, wearing day clothes more frequently, and regulating my diet to now maintain my weight as opposed to increase it), in a very realistic and horrifying light. Another milestone, but again not recognised as such at the time. I knew this next stage was going to be harder, and explained to the staff nurse who very kindly congratulated me on 'your success' that I saw it rather like learning to drive. When I had passed my test, I was not a driver, I was a beginner. Here now was the beginning – starting to live at a normal weight and in a normal way.

I can remember thinking how good that explanation sounded! And the staff nurse seemed to appreciate my attitude, but I'm afraid it was all bluff. I was desperately trying to convince myself that this was how I saw it, ignoring totally my fears and real feelings about what was to come. (The clinic's programme was very disciplined and timetabled so I knew exactly the next steps.) Possibly this, too, was a milestone – I *knew* I wasn't telling the real truth, as I *knew* I *had* jumped off those weighing scales in real and honest delight. In my time in the clinic, I was the only one to do this. Others fainted, cried, screamed or showed extreme disappointment. Perhaps, then, in those few euphoric moments there had been a glimpse of the real, positive Ann Cox. The 'low' destroying the 'high' was my anorexia, with which I was so used to coping with my feelings. There was nothing good about living, nine stones two pounds did not equate with any success. I was going to fail now, out on the road, having passed what I called my 'L-plate' stage. There was nothing about which to feel positive, and I went to bed very early indeed, knowing I was going to experience all sorts of crashes and traumas – and, hopefully, a fatality.

I was once referred to as a 'professional anorectic', and hence as a master of the art of deception. Self-deception, too, thus making me my own worst enemy, in the truest sense. Whichever way I looked, however positive I tried to be, I always put myself in a 'no-win' situation. Briefly, on that Sunday, I had thought, 'Terrific, I've made it'. Within eight hours, on the following Monday, I was thinking very differently indeed:

> *'I don't like my breasts, tummy and legs. I've never had a bust before, it's uncomfortable and gives a very unpleasant sensation when I walk or clean my teeth. It's also sore. I feel bigger than ever in day clothes. I'm no longer slim, just a huge, fat lump. When I walk, it all wobbles. I don't want all this fat. I don't think I want any feminine curves either. As a woman I look and feel a failure.'*
>
> (Logbook entry 4/6/90)

And subsequently throughout the following week:

> *'Socially I'm scraping by, but I have no humour and cannot laugh. Regarding womanly sexuality, if this is it, I loathe it. Last night I dreamt I was beautiful and desirable and thin. Physical relationships from now on are an impossibility. I couldn't bear a close relationship, I don't like my own body. I hate it.'*
>
> (Logbook entry 6/6/90)

> *'I don't want to get to know myself – I don't like myself. I want to leave here, (the clinic), I don't want to continue living. I couldn't go back to anorexia, that was too painful and too slow; I'm too fat now and I haven't got the patience to lose all this weight.'*
>
> (Logbook entry 7/6/90)

> *'There are too many problems in this world; living, sleeping, crying, talking, communicating, giving, receiving, remembering. I can't do any of them. Nor be Ann Cox. Who is she? I only know Ann Orexia and I hate both. Where is Pollyanna? my favourite*

69

childhood character. She always *saw the good in the bad, she was always playing the "glad game" and being positive. I'm not glad, there's nothing good. I want to die – and stop feeling.'*
(Logbook entry 9/6/90)

My own personal recovery process was, unfortunately, at this stage, compounded by physical complications, which, along with everything else, made the whole thing even more frightening. In the early stages of my admission, I had already experienced something of this; I didn't go to the toilet for four weeks, and peeing had also been difficult, these problems being a backlash from taking so many laxatives, suppositories and diuretics. Once reaching target weight and able to mobilise, meant being in a vertical position for most of the time, and this caused me to develop severe oedema, something which no doubt was there during the months I spent on bed rest, but which didn't manifest itself until I started moving. My legs and arms swelled considerably, becoming like tree trunks from knees to toes, and shoulders to fingers. Likewise my face ballooned, particularly around the eye area. The legacy of so many purgatives was quite violent, frightening – because my weight soared towards eleven stones – and extremely painful. My tissues did not know how to behave normally, being used only to severe dehydration. When I *did* take in any fluid they grabbed at it, soaking it up like a sponge (hence the quick weight gains when I was ill and drank after purging), and were continuing to do so, because they didn't know how to filter excess fluids through my body back to my kidneys. Thus everything stayed on board. I was literally getting bigger by the day and although I understood this was due to fluid retention, I still felt I was getting *fatter* by the day. All I could focus on was a comparison between how I was – at four stones – and now, nearly SEVEN stones heavier. My target weight was just above nine. I was not only a fat anorectic, I was OVERWEIGHT. Mobilising became almost impossible; pain killers and diuretics had no effect and the toilet difficulties recurred. X-rays showed up high impactions and I regularly had to have enemas in order to pass out the faeces. These were absolutely excruciating. Sometimes I felt better constipated, although the problem was not always for this reason. I was told that passing waste material through the body is firstly instigated by the stomach, which sorts out the waste products and produces the necessary bacteria for the matter to be eventually passed through to the lower bowel for excretion. It appeared that not only had my bowel muscles to regain their own power and control, but my stomach, too, had to be re-educated to induce the process. Body and mind gave up! The therapy at the same time, stirring up so many issues, feelings and emotions, I became more and more negative and depressed. I could not cope with it all. I wasn't prepared to. Neither would I let myself face up to, nor understand, what these feelings and emotions were. All my thoughts continued to be channelled through the old coping mechanism of food, weight, shape and size, and self-disgust and hatred concerning my body.

> 'What's the use? I'm so depressed. I haven't got the will to live with my shape. I have no point to living – no-one/nothing to love. I'm so terrified, I just don't want to be.'
>
> (Logbook entry 31/7/90)

> 'I can't live in this body. It's shameful, disgusting and disgraceful. I hate it. It looks so puffy and fat and gross. It TERRIFIES me. I felt desperate when I was 4 stones, suicidal – I feel even more desperate now.'
>
> (Logbook entry 5/8/90)

> 'I have nothing to offer. I'm lousy when it comes to communicating and socialising with others. It's impossible to relax and enjoy myself. There's too

71

much going on inside, plus the worry about how I look on the outside. I am so ugly and revolting. I'm terrified of my own sexuality. I feel repulsed by it, and I hate the bodily signs of womanhood as they reappear and get going again. Unwanted hair, under-arm and pubic areas, is growing at an alarming rate, I can't deal with it. It has not been there so so many years, nor has perspiring. (A body at a very low weight ceases to perspire in an effort to keep in all possible bodily warmth.) *Using anything feminine like perfumed soap, talcum powder, moisturiser and deodorant scares me a lot. I'm too terrified to use these things* (something else I hadn't thought to bring with me into the clinic), *I'm smelly and ugly now, and a disaster on all fronts. I'm a horrid person, I have no compassion, giving or caring in my nature.'*

(Logbook entry 14/8/90)

When the oedema had first become evident, I had been told by the professional experts that indeed this was not an uncommon problem. One that would disappear within a few days. As it did not, compounded by my worries and fears, I was, a week later, reassured that the problem should go within two to three weeks. Again it did not and I was horri-fied to be eventually told by the specialists who were 'impressed by the chronicity' (!) – I think they meant shocked – of my oedema, that they themselves were now at a loss as to what to do. The team of doctors and nurses were now very concerned that they 'might not be able to get it right'. As well as abject horror and mortification, my blood was also boiling at this stage and (perhaps another small milestone as I expressed my thoughts), I let go a string of angry comments, suggesting that they 'bloody well *had* to get it right'. They had got me into this predicament, they could get me out of it!

By the end of July (the 1990 summer being a long heat-wave), it was becoming fairly obvious that I was experiencing great difficulties with regard to personal care and hygiene. I couldn't bear to look at my body, nor touch it, so washing was only a lick, not even a promise. I hated it too much. Mirrors were distressing and traumatic, so hair drying, and styling were on the 'as good as a guess' basis again, and, in an effort to keep a low profile, I remained in one pair of black leggings and a white T-shirt, which I washed out overnight. Of course, I suppose I was all the more noticeable for this, but my line of thought was that it was better for people to think 'She never changes her clothes' rather than 'Goodness! doesn't her wardrobe look awful, she's so fat'. As my nightie and dressing-gown had been my daily 'uniform' until I reached target weight, so did these leggings and T-shirt become – for four and a half months. With help I eventually confessed to these problems (which also included washing of very personal items), and was given a programme to assist me. I also found a friend – a fellow patient – Sue, to help me, and Sue and I became stalwart friends, as are we today. It was not an easy programme to follow, but I started off with non-scented soaps, and deodorants, for example, and a 'grit my teeth and bear it attitude', with regard to touching and washing various parts of me. Many a tear was shed on Sue's shoulder, but I'm glad to say my shoulder became useful too. Sue had her own problems which she needed to share, and she and I, having enormous respect for one another, became each other's confidante.

Dealing with perspiration was not the only horror. Blushing and flushing were embarrassing, and as for vaginal discharge, I was at my wit's end, because along with this came sexual desires and dreams, all new to me, and something which made me certain I was perverse. I kept looking at other female patients and staff, looking at their feminine curves with admiration and sometimes envy, occasionally disgust, mixed with dreaming of affairs with the male doctors and nurses. Being certain that relationships with men would never be a part of my life though, I was not motivated into better personal care, simply more disgusted and repulsed by myself and my thoughts.

73

'I'll do anything and everything to get rid of these feminine bits of me. They're not curves like other people's! Just lumps and bumps. My leggings are showing signs of wear at the crotch where my legs rub together. It's revolting. Sometimes I long for a party dose of laxatives, or to vomit – perhaps it will all go away then, or at least numb my feelings for a while.'

(Logbook entry 22/8/90)

For a short while the urge to vomit after each meal and snack became a great temptation, but one which through sheer determination, with perhaps a little of 'What's the use now, I'm too fat, it won't make any difference' attitude, I did avoid. Instead I continued to spew out into my logbook.

'Caring for myself is frightening and problematic. Every morning I'm frightened to get up, and once up I long to be back in my nightie, and look forward to the dark and getting under the covers.'

(Logbook entry 22/8/90)

'I slept too much last night. I've got so much energy with which to hate myself this morning. I long to hurt myself.'

(Logbook entry 23/8/90)

'Hips, tummy, thighs, bottom and breasts cause such an ugly sensation. They wobble about. The sensations scare me. Eating an apple and cleaning my teeth make me more aware of my breasts. They seem so ugly. I hoped femininity meant daintiness. There would be a defined female form and outline, not all this flab. I was hiding behind something when I was thin (I had yet to realise that something was my own true identity), *I'm sure hidden now. ALL THIS FAT. It just makes me want to hide, because, when I was thin, I was obviously poorly, but fat demands*

74

living and coping, laughing and talking and being someone.'

(Logbook entry 24/8/90)

I felt a very lonely being in that clinic within my fat body, despite my friendship with Sue, and contact with fellow patients and nursing staff. Barely able to walk I was now shuffling along with legs clad in tight tubi-grip, only able to use trodden down old slippers, because of hypersensitive hot spot areas on my feet. I was refused any walking aids – anorexia had been a crutch, I was not going to be presented with nor allowed another one – and my only reasons for now staying in the hospital was that I was convinced (i) I would not be accepted in the community, nor could I manage so incapacitated, and (ii) I had no right to a place in the outside world, I had no identity, I was a nobody and a nothing. The world was living, but as far as I was concerned I thought my world was irrevocably dead. I had killed it. The road to recovery I saw only as punitive with a capital P. There was immense mental and physical pain now, and again the longing to die was uppermost in my thoughts:

When this life seems just like a waste of time,
Is trying to escape from it such a crime?
The crime is in living
– I'd rather be DEAD.
I hate me so much – from my toes to my head.
Pretending I can cope – just – when I'm sad,
Having to convince others that I'm glad,
Glad to be alive with them today, when all I want
   is to get away,
– hide in the dark,
Never see this body of mine.
Not to be touched.
– I hate me too much.
Whilst time and life go eternally on and on
All the time, I just wish that I was gone
– to another world, but – to start once more,

75

To try and end this personal, internal war?
You see I'm fed up with fighting –
I hate all of life.
I'd like to get at it, to slash with a knife
The thoughts, fears and shadows that follow me
   round
– that now, very soon, will drive me into the
   ground.

(Logbook entry 22/8/90)

On the morning of that particular day, after a seven day period of not having been to the toilet again, I was given four enemas in a row, but with no result. This increased my feelings of desperation and at 4.00 p.m. another entry in my logbook read: 'Suicide. I'm going'.

I went to supper that evening, at 6.00 p.m. planning to abscond as soon as I could. Despite my poor mobility I managed to get out into the hospital grounds where there was a bus stop and caught a local bus to the train station. There, I purchased a platform ticket and sat on the station, timing the slow and fast through trains. I did not want anyone to see a big drama, nor did I want too many people in the way. After twenty minutes I knew my plan and waited for the next fast through train. As I heard it coming I went to the edge of the platform and threw myself off. However, the hospital having noticed my absence, had notified the police, and unbeknown to me, they had been observing me. As I launched myself off the platform, so three policemen jumped after me, pushing me off the line as the train rushed through, running over one of my slippers, one policeman's hat and another's truncheon. I struggled as best as I could, but again I did not succeed in killing myself. If I had, as was made plain to me, quite possibly the four of us would have died, but that fact provoked no pang of conscience, nor shock, only anger. Anger at not being dead, at not being allowed to die. I was returned to the clinic, under escort, and immediately sectioned, with a view to being transferred to another psychiatric hospital. My mental state they consid-

76

ered to be beyond their help. I would never recover from anorexia. I was too ill.

Ironically it was that opinion – that I was too ill – that was the turning point for me. Instead of resigning my thoughts to agreeing with this viewpoint, I decided I was not too ill, that I *was* going to recover and that Ann Cox was going to leave Ann Orexia behind. So instead of regarding the section, which now involved being 'specialled', (ie, twenty four hour surveillance for fear of further suicide attempts), as a punishment I saw it as a relief, a sort of safety net from acting on my thoughts, and as a reason to start being positive. I started playing Pollyanna's 'glad game', and was astonished to find it was quite easy. I felt I knew the trigger of that suicide attempt – not the fact that the hospital had told me they didn't know if they could 'get it (the oedema) right', but that along with this they had also told me there was a chance that even after twenty two years of being without periods, menstruation might restart. Something else, just like boobs developing, that I hadn't even considered. At the back of my mind, since my hair had started re-growing, and my cramps, heart, blood, breathing and sight problems had all resolved themselves, I actually believed that the oedema would also go, so this was no real problem however, as for periods – no way!

I had to resolve and try to understand my feelings regarding womanhood, femininity and my own sexuality. Having identified these particular areas, I then recalled the former words of the psycho-therapist I had seen in my last admission in Brighton – 'Use me'. Finally I understood the meaning behind them. With great commitment, I wrote at length in my logbook, sometimes several times a day. I used it to capacity. If I got stuck on a subject or topic, I asked myself why. Why did I feel such and such? Why should I hate myself? Each member of staff who specialled me I talked to. In therapy classes I talked about myself at long last, instead of just listening to others, and my art work became an abstract expression of my emotions.

All these positive movements gradually started leading

towards greater self-confidence and self-awareness. I was becoming positive with a capital 'P', and at long last, with the help of my individual therapist, Aurélie, I opened up, found the liar in me, found the honesty in me and hung on to every feeling and emotion, in order that I could express it constructively, instead of through food and/or bodily obsession and abuse. I was determined now not to see recovery as punitive. It might be painful, but I was going to be Positive, and I added another category to my logbook – 'Anything good'. I vowed to find something good about which to write every day. My logbook became my best friend; I told it everything and I realised there was no point in lying to it. Recovery demanded openness and honesty, and via my logbook I was determined to be an 'open book' in order to achieve this.

> '*Something has really changed – the intensity behind the degree of hate and terror has decreased considerably. The depression seems to be lifting. It's a new feeling. I've never felt that there is a future for me without anorexia nervosa, but now this relief has brought optimism. I've found compassion for others too, and some kinder feeling towards myself. I just know I'm going to make it.*'
>
> (Logbook entry 26/8/90)

A blackness, a void –
But there is colour ahead.
Confusion and doubt –
Surely it's the way out?
I've got to work hard,
Strip myself, open up.
Turn shame into anger
And see guilt like a cup.
It's full at the moment,
Overflowing in fact –
But it could gently be emptied,
And I'd be out of the trap.

You'd have to sip slowly –
I'm already so drained,
And it's still pouring over –
But it can be contained.
I'll leave this blackness behind,
Find something whole for the void,
The shadows must go,
And the Voice left behind.
My prison doors will be opened
– one day I'll be free,
Caring so much for such a lot
– but most of all – FOR ME.
The table will be laid
And I'll be ready to eat,
– to enjoy – at last, the banquet.
Oh! what a treat!

(Logbook entry 27/8/90)

It seemed at this point, although I was not totally aware of all that was going on, a lot of salient milestones had been passed. I had finally admitted to, and accepted, my problem, that it was not just a peculiar attitude towards food, nor simply the deadly pursuit of thinness. It was something over which I had no control, but which I could regain, with help – for example, food and eating re-education, and therapy to look beyond the physical symptoms, in order to try and unearth the deeply buried emotional underlying issues. I realised recovery was to involve self-examination and self-analysis through the various mediums of talking, art work, and psycho-drama, even though it might at times be a hell that seemed worse than my eating disorder. It was a paradox that the failure of my final attempt to die marked my decision to live. Possibly I had no choice but to live, but I decided my life was not going to be one encompassing any eating disorder, nor would it be spent in another psychiatric hospital, and, like a bolt of lightning, I knew I had to change my attitude towards therapy and recovery. However hard I had tried, I had still been channelling everything through weight, shape and size. (Food too, sometimes, if I ate it quickly, for example, or shovelled it down.) I had continually felt that I was being punished for being ill, ie, being made FAT.

This being the turning point, recovery became all about meeting challenges, taking risks in talking about various traumas and events in my life and most important of all, hanging on to my feelings in order that I might experience them and examine them. I began to realise that living was all about experiencing feelings, *NOT* solving them.

I guess another sort of key for me was now seeing recovery as a challenge. As a PE teacher and a sports person myself, I always performed to win. The same with anorexia. Even if I won a tennis match or gymnastic competition, it was never good enough. Likewise with anorexia, I was never thin enough. I decided that I was now tired of not being good enough, and seeing life only through the eyes of failing. I was going to win for once! And that approach to winning became my new challenge. Finally I inverted all that energy channelled into anorexia, and self-destruction, and reversed it into coming up the other way – to beat the eating disorder despite the battle royals that might ensue.

My determined approach and changed attitude of mind being evident to one and all, the clinic decided against transferring me elsewhere, and after ten days of specialling me, announced I could stay. I was really and truly delighted and overjoyed, and began to see the clinic and staff as friends, not enemies. They were offering me the trusting and supportive environment needed to help re-build my self-esteem, confidence and respect. I could take it or leave it. I chose to take it. I grabbed it! I used it! And took a completely different attitude to talking and writing about myself. Until recently I had seen it as totally selfish, but I began to realise that a lot of talking about oneself and one's feelings is necessary, albeit, at times, a somewhat self-centered approach. I had simply used the guilt caused by constant talking and thinking about myself as yet another excuse to stop thinking. Now, I realised, as I looked at fellow patients, that I did not begrudge them talking about themselves, so why should I, myself? If it clarified a person, gave a life and a future, then it could only be good. Good for them and good for me. And good it was going to be!

> 'My attitude towards my sexuality is improving I think. Also I've been spending more time with other patients, and I no longer feel uncomfortable socially. They seem to accept and/or like me. I think I'm beginning to accept me too. Perhaps one day I'll even like myself. Sometimes, feeling so positive, I feel I'm on cloud 9; I will be able to wear nice clothes – trousers, dresses, skirts, blouses and I'll look OK, then suddenly I fall off my cloud with a bump. Doubt creeps in as I catch sight of my ugly fat face, fat legs, broad chest, and muscular arms, and terror, too, begins to manifest itself.'

> (Logbook entry 31/8/90)

A woman with feelings,
Wanting to feel – but too frightened to allow them.
Not certain of a future –
No love to give or receive,
No-one there to give to or receive from.
But this woman – ME – is real,
– and she wants to be real,
Not locked up in that prison
– like the child restricted to her room.
Let me out! –
I want to be proud to be free.
I'll take you by the hand
– and you'll think 'What a pleasant lady'.
Not the vile horrid bitch – my shadow that follows
*   me around.*
You'll think 'Hey! Here's someone!'
– and yes! I will be someone,
Proud enough to walk tall and be me,
And sit down to the table with the graces of a
*   woman*

81

– who is liked, respected and accepted,
And above all, likes herself.

(August 1980)

Although I had developed a lot of determination, I also had a lot of doubt, and was still using the words 'fat' and 'thin'. There were also times, too, when I felt it be all too much, and looked backwards to the 'old days', instead of forwards, to the new, to try to find and accept my new self and identity. Having considered myself a nothing and a nobody, because I just didn't know who I was or what I really felt and thought, it wasn't easy recognising that I was a somebody. I experienced great disappointment when I lapsed into backward glances, but hard thinking, and self-analysis, provided me with being able to accept this as 'normal', not failing. I obviously needed, and had, to mourn and grieve for my anorexia/bulimia. Just as does the wife who loses her husband, and gets lost in thoughts of their time together, so I had to experience the time my eating disorder and I had spent together. Mourning and grieving a person's death are natural and normal processes in order to go forward, to a future, so I thus concluded that mourning and grieving the death of my anorexia/bulimia natural and normal too.

I found writing to be my greatest and most valuable outlet. My logbook could be used twenty four hours a day, seven days a week, and we had a very personal and private relationship. No-one had to read it, although I could show the nursing staff entries if I wanted to, so I could put everything in it. And I did – my most confidential thoughts and feelings went down. I told it everything. I confessed everything. Honesty and truthfulness were absolutely necessary. During my illness, and before it, I had lied in an effort to establish confidence and respect from others. There had been so much wanting, wanting, wanting, from other people, because I had no self-worth/respect/esteem/confidence, but I could not get this from my logbook, I couldn't impress it; it couldn't talk back nor show any reaction, but what it did do was to become my reflection. A reflection of the *inside* me.

82

Everything put down in black and white made my thoughts real. As I wrote in it, and re-read my entries, I gradually got to know myself. It became a mirror of my inner thoughts, and physical mirrors having been a very important part of my life during my illness (to see if I was thin enough), it seemed obvious that this new sort of mirror should become such an important medium now.

I adopted the 'no gain without pain' attitude, and persevered with much dedication, and I gradually discovered that my life was constructed around an intricate collection of problems and traumas that I had been unable to face and which, therefore, through anorexia, I had actually managed to push away so far that I had forgotten them, because at the time I had been unable to cope with, or confront, them. Personal and relationship problems had been bypassed and 'put on ice', so that they didn't have to be looked into seriously. Unearthing everything and examining my feelings, and acknowledging both, caused many tears and much sadness, but through the low feelings came the smiles and laughter, too.

> *'Someone has said what a lovely smile and sense of humour I've got! Me! Aren't people nice.'*
> (Logbook entry 31/8/90)

> *'I've just cracked a joke! We've all been crying from laughing, so much. How nice to have tummy-ache from a belly laugh, instead of from 200 laxatives and several suppositories.'*
> (Logbook entry 1/9/90)

As I let my feelings surface, so coincidentally did the oedema begin to suddenly shift, and as well as using the mirror of my logbook, I also started to use, with trained help, the mirror in the bathroom, in an effort to see and accept the outside me as well as the inside me. I felt I *was* winning, but within that positive frame of mind I made a big mistake, I thought I could do everything at once and typical of me tried to run before I could walk. As a result, of course, I gave myself a few more hard knocks and bruises! My mother had always accused me of learning the hard way, and here I was, at it again! I was advised to slow down, to take one aspect of all this newness, and one day at a time. To start looking at some achievements, instead of only always wanting to achieve more. And was that hard work – slowing down! I sometimes wished I worked on clockwork, so that I could just partly wind myself up to go more slowly, but of course this, too, was part of the therapy – learning one's limitations, learning when to stop, when to push on, and how to be one's master and friend at the same time.

As I learned to slow down, however, so environmental and physical changes speeded up! And I remember thinking how unfair that it should 'never rain, only pour', now, whilst I was trying to go more slowly. This too, though, was to become a valuable learning experience – one could not, and cannot, – have control over everything.

The main physical and environmental changes that came all at once were threefold. The fluid loss, as the oedema went, resulted in almost three stones of weight loss! In as nearly as few weeks the pains in my legs became much worse and my mobility poorer, and I had a 'show' of coloured discharge, indicating that periods returning were a real probability, instead of a vague possibility. I was therefore now sixteen pounds underweight, barely able to walk and very definitely all woman! Everything combined into another nightmare, with more doubts.

What is me? – what do I really look like now?
Who am I? – what do I really feel, now?
I'm thin again, but I'm no longer dying to be thin
– just slim,
– if that's me now, that's Ann.
All I want is to look good and feel nice,
I'm sure I will,
I'm sure I'll get there,
– I want to, so I know I will.

84

But why can't I walk?
And why is it hard again, to talk?
I'm determined to go on, persevere and face the
*   images in the mirror*
I'll look hard for the true reflections
And leave the guilt, shame and hatred behind.
I'm a winner, I know it!
Look at all this – just blow it!
SMILE Ann, laugh and talk,
To yourself, talk and smile
Make sure to keep on this road, EVERY damn
*   mile.*

(Logbook entry 14/9/90)

Nevertheless, having now adopted Pollyanna's thinking and positive attitude, I adopted another two 'Ps' – Perseverence and Persistence, and hung on to optimism with gritted teeth. I was certain things were 'going to be right', and more important still, entries in my logbook were now including ones showing higher self-esteem and self-regard, even though I did wonder constantly if normality was for me, if I could be a normal member of the general community, the outside world.

> *'Shit to my shape! What the hell does it matter? As long as I'm free from anorexia nervosa – and I will be! – free to enjoy what life has to offer, and free, too, to give something of myself. I feel more feminine, I feel I might look OK and inside I'm FEELING. FEELING OK. I may feel fat, I know I have to substitute another word, an emotion and today that word is "OK". I only feel fat because I'm quite scared of feeling OK, of now being able to cope with normal things, albeit slowly, like personal hygiene, and being a liked and respected woman by my fellow patients, and, I think, the staff.'*

(Logbook entry 25/9/90)

Being in such a persevering frame of mind, I continued to mobilise despite the excruciating pain, which I described like 'red hot pins sticking into all my bones from my lower back down', and worked harder still at using all the available mediums for hanging on to feelings and expressing them. I was determined I could leave food-abuse and self-abuse behind, that I could be a something and a somebody without them, that there was a place in the world for me, and a ME, an identity, for the world. I was aware that my weight, having gone down, was simultaneous with better feelings about myself too, and knowing how I had tricked and deceived myself in the past, I seriously thought about the significance of this. I concluded that it was not because I was feeling thin again. In fact at eight stones, I was terrified of losing more weight, because, firstly, I was frightened that once into the seven stone bracket, I would want the six and then the five stone brackets and so on (ie, the line of thought I had had for so many years), and secondly, I actually didn't want to lose what I'd got – an identity and a self-awareness. This took a lot of soul-searching, but I was certain I was being truthful to myself and hence, when the clinic suggested that once again I was coping with my feelings via weight loss, ie, anorexia nervosa, I challenged them. I felt angry at their suggestion and so positive about my own decision that I vented both in one particular ward round. My weight loss was not due to cheating regarding my food intake, it was due quite simply to the oedema going. All through my hospital period I had given the medics my trust and accepted their control. Now it was time for *them* to trust *me* and accept *my* control!

Perhaps it sounds odd to say that the various physical complications and, finally, the pain and great difficulty walking, seemed to help me discover an inner resource, but they did. Pollyanna was really working – finding the good in the bad and turning negative experiences into positive ones. The more positive experiences I discovered, the more positive I was that my world was not, after all, irrevocably dead. I knew it was alive and that I could breathe life into it. The latter complication also appeared to provide me with a different dimension, a different way of feeling and seeing things – almost a pathway to acceptance. Acceptance of the outside me and the inner me. However, at the beginning of October came another hurdle, which I elected to be my last. The medical team, still seemingly ignoring my pain, and only concentrating on my weight loss, announced that they considered me only as anorexic. I would have to go back on full bed rest to gain the necessary sixteen pounds – to get to what now seemed to me, to be the 'be all and end all', target weight. If the pain continued I was advised that I could have a referral to a pain clinic in order to come to terms with it.

I was shocked, horrified, disgusted and indignant, all in one go. The team had always made it clear that target weight was not something which might make one feel at one's best, nor look best, live longest or whatever, but was the weight at which one stood the best chance of avoiding the emotional and physical costs of anorexia nervosa. I cried out, strong and loud, that perhaps they had to reconsider this view. Surely it couldn't be a standard equation applicable to everyone? I was coping inside, but outside I was in agony. I felt the team had to see its own imperfections and own up to them. After all, they did say they weren't perfect, as well as having earlier voiced to me their doubts about 'getting it right'. I told them that it seemed to me they now epitomised the media which, when they couldn't see anything wrong assumed nothing was, or could be, wrong.

The media looks at the thin anorectic and knows something is amiss, but regarding the person suffering bulimia, who usually looks quite acceptable, are reluctant to accept that they too have a problem. I was now in a similar situation. I looked, to the average person, to be quite normal, weight-wise, but I was in pain; pain being something that, unfortunately, is not a measurable or definable quantity/entity. The team felt they knew better – because whatever my appearance, they knew my weight and knew that I was underweight. I knew differently. I was experiencing extreme pain and *I* knew something else was wrong. Being a 'doer' and a 'trier' I had mobilised to the best of my ability and, I felt, had coped reasonably well and in a constructive way, with the physical complications. I felt, though, that perhaps all I had done was prove to everyone what I could do, rather than the physical agony I was in. Perhaps I should stop trying to walk. After all, it hurt like hell, and I often fell over. Perhaps I should refuse to try. Perhaps I should shout, scream or cry all the time. Perhaps, perhaps, but NO! I told the team I wasn't going to do that, but that in order to be fair to me they ought to allow a second opinion as regards the physical pain.

As a result of this, my feelings and wishes were respected, and although I certainly felt unhappy about having to prove I was telling the truth whilst the various tests were being carried out, I continued to use all the mediums of expression in a constructive way, particularly my logbook, in which I thrashed out much. As many as six or seven entries were made each day/night. I continued, too, to mobilise to the best of my ability and am very glad I did. I found the beauty of nature. Not being able to sleep for long because of the discomfort, I used to get up in the mornings, around 6.00 a.m., along with the morning dawn, and go for a walk before breakfast. With few people around, and the beautiful sunrises sending out a warm pink glow, I discovered wild flowers, squirrels, and birds, along with acorns and beautiful brown smooth conkers, all of which provided me with the title for this book. I began to realise what I had missed during those years of my illness – a very beautiful world, one in which I sensed much tranquillity and inner peace and a sense of being a part of something. This became self-perpetuating in that I wanted more and more to be alive and well in the world, and it also gave me incentive to cope with such aspects as learning to cook and cater for myself with the help of the dietician (my! did she have a lot of patience with me) and come to terms with my new shape and new feelings. Not just to simply sweep them under the carpet, but rather let them surface in order that they might be acknowledged, and then be put aside, no longer posing a threat. The world and living seemed very welcoming; there was so much about which to be thankful. Living with an eating disorder had been such a waste of time. I vowed anorexia/bulimia nervosa would soon be a past chapter in my history.

When the results of the tests came through it was obvious that I had been telling the truth. For that I was glad, but very upset to learn that I was now carrying the legacy for all the years of chronic starvation and laxative abuse. My hip and leg bones were cracked, fractured and split and they might well crumble; I was now registered as physically disabled.

At this point came the great divide and differing viewpoints regarding my situation. On the one hand those who had carried out the tests considered my target weight might be too heavy for my back, hips and legs to carry, thus causing further pain and greater disability, whilst the eating disorder specialists considered that anything other than nine stones two pounds pointed to being anorexic.

I urged for a compromise to be agreed; if one said eight stones and the other nine stones plus, what about eight and a half stones? The team, however, were adamant; I had signed a contract, upon admission, which had involved getting to, and maintaining, the set target weight. Any breach of contract, whatever the circumstances, it seemed, could not be considered. I was thus faced with further choice (choice being something which had always been a difficult issue, and often is with anyone suffering an eating disorder, because allowing oneself anything is just not on). Go up to nine stones two pounds and maybe even face life unable to walk at all, or leave the clinic – to either die or cope.

I chose the latter, but again, in order to make sure I was really making the right decision, my logbook took a big bashing. I, also, for the three days' grace I was given to make my decision, took a big risk and broke all the clinic's rules. A touch of the old obstinacy and stubbornness, perhaps, but a rebellion which proved to be very constructive and for which I was thankful I did still have a streak of obstinacy, although I would prefer to call it out and out assertiveness!

I refused to eat any of the hospital meals, and boycotted all the group therapy sessions (this with the agreement of the other patients involved). I was certain I wanted to leave the clinic – to cope and live without anorexia/bulimia nervosa, but I had to find out about living and life in the community. In those three days I went shopping – to buy food and look at food, (to see what was around to cook, and whether or not I would feel the urge, again, to starve or binge) and also to purchase new clothes. I was pleasantly astonished to discover that none of these new tasks proved overly difficult although mobilising was extremely painful and difficult at times, and, in fact, I quite enjoyed myself. I resolved to set my own target weight between eight stones two pounds and eight stones four pounds, and on the second of these three days discovered I had, through my own catering, gained a little weight – up to eight stones one pound. There was only one more thing to do – to discuss my resolve to leave with my girlfriend's parents, Pam and Ron Hedges, who over the years had, off and on, acted in loco parentis – and might be able to offer an objective viewpoint.

Between us, Pam, Ron and I felt that leaving the clinic was the best thing to do. Pam, in particular, felt I was well along the road to recovery, and I, for my part, despite niggling self-doubts, (because anorectic behaviour and thought patterns had been a part of my life for so long), was absolutely certain that I was ready for the next stage in the healing process. I thus announced my decision to the medical team, and we mutually agreed that I could leave, there thus being no need for either side to sign discharge papers. My fellow patients acknowledged my decision with consider-able admiration, and gave me a terrific send-off – lots of presents, cards and hugs. Having originally thought that we would all be spending Christmas together, the night before I left we pulled crackers and I gave them all little gifts. The following morning, on 19th October, 1990, Pam and Ron came to collect me to take me to their home in Bournemouth for a couple of weeks recuperation before I returned to my flat in Brighton. There were a lot of tears amongst the farewells, including the staff, oddly enough, and although I felt sad saying goodbye, I felt immense relief. My tears were a mixture of joy and sadness, but as I stepped out into the warm autumn sunshine, on a morning when I had seen a most breathtaking sunrise, joy had the upper hand. I knew I was ready to leave. Ready for that next stage which I decided to call my journey of discovery.

MY JOURNEY OF DISCOVERY

Having left hospital, on 19th October 1990 trying to believe, as I vividly recall, that anorexia/bulimia nervosa really were behind me forever, I suppose my journey of discovery began the next day, on 20th October. On the evening of the 19th, in Bournemouth, in a lovely home which represented love, warmth and non-institutionalism, I wrote in my logbook an entry that highlighted both my certainties and doubts.

> *'Food is no longer a problem. Looking ahead is – it's all so unknown. Will I ever be able to cope with returning to my own flat eventually, and living on my own? Will anorexia or suicide become too strong a temptation again? I want to have a proper niche in life and feel and be needed and wanted. I want and need to give of myself too. Giving and receiving; living, loving and laughing, these are my new hopes and goals, but are they just dreams? I'm certain I have too much to hang on to within me that is good to let my determination slip, but I'm so wary. For such a long period in my life I've been so clever at kidding myself.'*

Coming out of hospital and stepping into a normal home was a wonderful and very emotional moment for me. For so many years, all I had known were the four walls of various hospitals, or the four walls of my own flat, which had been places only for force-feeding, starving, bingeing, vomiting or purging. I had never felt, despite having had my own property, that I had ever had a home such as the dictionary defines it; 'a residence dear to one' (*Collins English Dictionary*). Home for me was wherever I was hanging my hat at the time. It was somewhere that had walls, a floor, a roof and windows; it never gave me a feeling of security, pleasure, comfort or warmth. Wherever I happened to be was just another prison cell, epitomising the prison cell of my eating disorder. However, Pam and Ron's home felt to me to be a very beautiful place; it gave me a very warm glow, and I cried on seeing the lovely bedroom they had made up for me. I cried too when I saw the bathroom, so clean and fresh, no vomit or excreta stains on their carpet or walls, no medicine chests full of laxatives, diuretics and strong drugs. Best of all was the kitchen – a proper kitchen with all the usual utensils and store cupboards holding food and baking ingredients, and a fridge and freezer full of goodies that no longer scared me. No longer would I be stuffing food down as if there was no tomorrow. There was no need; I considered food as a friend now, and a necessity for living and being healthy. I was also learning to enjoy it. Within the long months of my final hospital confinement I had purposely chosen to go without condiments or sauces of any kind. I knew I had to find out about the different foods and their tastes; I needed to know what I liked and what I didn't, and which were my preferences, and that had proved a very valuable step. I already knew I loved omelettes, cheese and peanut butter sandwiches and that I wasn't too keen on tinned mushy peas or fish that had been battered!

Friday evenings for Pam and Ron were, (and remained) 'night-off-in-the-kitchen-nights', ie, fish and chips from the local chippy was the menu, and 19th October was a Friday. Pam, bless her, had anticipated that perhaps this particular Friday would mean some cooking, and she had also stocked the fridge with lots of low calorie foods. (And why not? – after all she had never known me eat anything more than a few calories, apart from a few binges I had on Yorkie Bars which I had stolen from their larder). On opening the fridge and faced with that still very scary thing 'choice', the tears flowed again. I didn't want to still be associated with low-cal, non-fattening stuff; I wanted to be normal. So between us, Pam and I decided upon a cheese omelette for me that evening, with a portion of chips from the chippy, from whence Ron usually made their purchase, and I, at the same time decided on a rule of 'no forbidden foods'. That Friday, I'm proud to say, was the only evening I had anything different from Pam and Ron. Friday nights became fish and chip nights for me, too, although I did opt for the fish fried in breadcrumbs. I didn't, don't and probably never will like battered fish simply because of the taste, calories don't matter one iota.

Whilst Pam and Ron stopped after the first course (eaten of course, the right way – out of the paper, and with fingers!), I went on to have a pudding, as I always did, and later on, before bed, I enjoyed coffee and one plain and one chocolate biscuit. I had learned a lot in hospital, once receptive to it, regarding food and how much was necessary to maintain my weight, as well as learning the values of different foods and what constituted a balanced diet. The low-calorie products that Pam had purchased especially for me remained in the fridge for a very long time. In fact, the tubs of cottage cheese had to be thrown out because they grew a blue coat; likewise the skimmed milk and natural yoghurts! I did use up some of the diet yoghurts, mainly because of the obvious trouble and expense to which Pam had gone, but these on things like sponges and fruit crumbles, instead of custard, and these sweets became known within the 'family' as 'heavies'. I had found it necessary within a week's menus to have three heavy puddings (such as sponge and custard), two medium, (for example rice) and one light (fruit or ice cream). I also knew what a proper portion regarding a main meal should be, (for example eight ounces of potato (two scoops if mashed) or four ounces if with a carbohydrate such as pastry or pasta). Hence every evening up went the cry 'portion time' from the kitchen, where Pam was about to dish up, followed by Ron's echo a few minutes later, 'heavy, medium or light then tonight?'!!

We laughed a lot together in those early days and we learned a lot, too. Pam and Ron learned much about eating disorders and the necessity to no longer wrap me up in cotton wool and protect me, but rather act as a support and guide. I, on the other hand, learned much about life and living and normality and I joined in the Hedges' social life to the full, finding my strengths and weaknesses, and to my astonishment, my ability to communicate with others and be a friend. Although my logbook was full of doubt, I felt I was doing reasonably well. Pam and Ron, I later gathered, had reservations, although they too were astonished at where I was at. I think they had expected me to still be obsessed about what I ate, regarding the calories, anyway, and how much and when. Their greatest fear, apparently, lay in the fact that I was unable to laugh at myself; I was too serious and any comical remark I might make about myself reeked of sarcasm. Hence, until that point, there was also a great deal of crying too, and as Ron said in his speech at my wedding a year later, (he acted as father of the bride): '...at first there were more tears than laughter ... more downs than ups'.

For me, though, the downs Ron spoke of were nothing like the downs and the depression which I had experienced over most of the last thirty eight years, and for me that meant progress, and I think, kept Pollyanna, positive thinking and determination to the fore. I was determined this journey was going to be a successful one. After all, painstaking though it was, I had travelled the road to recovery.

> *I've found the way out, and now I'll go further*
> *Through the murk and the fog, I'll even find fun.*
> *– I'll cry too, and laugh, but oh I'll enjoy!*
> *And I'll give myself permission one day to smile*
> *– to emerge smiling through all the ups and downs.*
> *The guilt will die – hard,*
> *But once it goes, I'll be able to give more, and*
> *   receive*
> *– Allow myself to receive.*

The void will be filled, the vessel, this body,
  acceptable,
And I shall like and be liked,
Be a friend and have friends,
Walk tall and be proud, proud of living and proud
  of me,
Proud to be a woman – who might even find love.
Who will face that banquet with relish, the day I
  join the table,
Join my friends, as a friend, who from the heart, is
  at last able.

(Logbook 21/10/90)

My determination to make anorexia/bulimia nervosa history was obviously there, but the old enemy, self-doubt, constantly reared its head, making me wonder if all my hopes were just pipe-dreams, or, worse still, whether anorexia was still around, and I was just kidding myself once again that I was the one in control. I made sure to continue writing in my logbook, and also in a diary I had been given as one of my leaving presents from the other hospital patients in the clinic. In this way I was able to continue the process of self-analysis and see the inside me reflected in black and white. Continuing to write in this manner was, I feel, the most important thing I did, and I wrote daily, dedicated entirely to discovering more about who I was, how I felt and why. The logbook I gave over to the more serious analytical logging of my thoughts and feelings, and the diary – a 'Winnie-the-Pooh' one, held the more light-hearted daily happenings. As a child I had been brought up with Winnie-the-Pooh, and I loved him as much as I did Pollyanna. Not so childish as one might think, because as with copying Pollyanna's glad game, I admired, and hung on to Winnie's theology of life. He was glad just to be. I was learning to be just that – and I also loved honey too!

When self-doubt was around good and strong, I found it very hard to work on any self-esteem. I tended to believe my doubts, rather than my goals, and for a while Pam and Ron

96

acted as my self-esteem. Pam, in particular, emphasised her belief in me, and her continued support in this area actually encouraged and motivated me to find my self-esteem by myself. After all, this was as she put it, being normal, and so it is. We all experience ups and downs, and like it or not it is generally up to us whether we swim or we sink. With Pam I would go back over all that I achieved, and we would set new goals – such as taking more control of the weekly shopping and, later, preparing some of the family meals. This not only gave Pam and Ron more 'night-off-in-the-kitchen' nights, but also encouraged me to take full responsibility for catering for myself, learn about various foods, learn to cook, and learn to produce normal size, nutritional meals.

Cooking was an area in which I was a real novice, and in those early days we ate several 'mystery sloshes'! They were never unpalatable, but they didn't always turn out looking like they should – shepherd's pie, for example! However, the one thing that was always cooked and hot were the plates! Ron will vouch for that. He experienced many a reddened hand in an attempt to carry his meal to the table, where we would sit, our conversation almost drowned out by the sizzling food which, if it hadn't cooked earlier on, was certainly doing so now! Then the sizzling would be drowned out by our laughter. At first, of course, I laughed from embarrassment, but Ron was the one who taught me what a belly-laugh was all about. Suddenly I found myself crying from laughter and because I was happy. I cried too, when I was sad, and for a while seemed to be in an awful muddle with regard to expressing my feelings. The amount of tears I was shedding made bailing out a real probability, and along with my efforts every morning to toast my bread to my liking (I do like it well done), thus filling the house with a blue, smelly haze and setting off the smoke alarms, we also had to consider many an evacuation!

The circumstances under which I had left the clinic meant that I had to forego the one to two year weekly follow-up counselling sessions with my individual therapist. The clinic's policy recognises that leaving them behind, and trying to live a new life without food abuse, creates new problems. They therefore consider follow-up therapy an absolute necessity; one, to check that target weights are being maintained, and two, to act as a support when facing problems and difficulties in day-to-day, normal living.

I had nothing, and one of the doctors, who patently disagreed with my decision to leave, had told me on the eve of my departure that he wouldn't be surprised if he was to hear I was dead within the week. That remark, however he meant it, provided me with yet another challenge, (perhaps therein being the reason he said it to me). I remember at the time thinking, 'What a daft twit. You wait!' And he's still waiting, as he will forever. However, I must have given off something of my disgust at his remark, in my manner, or appearance, that made him possibly think differently, because it was fifteen or twenty minutes later, as I passed the staff room, that I heard him say to one of the medical team, 'She'll make it...'

Now just who that 'she' was, I have to be honest and say I don't really know, but I took it as read that it was me. And with a smile of satisfaction, along with a two-fingered gesture, I continued past the staff-room, my only sorrow being that if I was indeed that 'she', he had been unable to make that encouraging remark to me. However, the clinic knew their stuff and knew how I looked upon everything positively as a challenge over which, however hard, I would win.

During the first weekend in Bournemouth, I realised just how shaky I was, both physically and mentally. Barely and only painfully being able to walk I no longer had structure to my day. For the past eighteen months, daily routines had been those of the hospital's. There had been regular meal-times, regular weighing sessions, regular therapy classes and always other patients to whom I could talk or to whom I could turn for company, or challenge to a game of Scrabble. I had had little in the way of responsibilities and, quite frankly, was very unsure about being able to cope in a responsible way with all my 'spare' time. It very suddenly felt like a case of having been eleven years old going on thirty eight, and I felt that I needed to plan aims, goals, routines and other indulgences to help me avoid the dreadful floundering feelings. I decided to join Pam and Ron in their church and voluntary work activities, which thus enabled me to build up a wonderful circle of new friends, and also, when possible, go with them to all their social functions, regardless of how intimidated I might feel, whether out for a meal, or to meet new people. I also decided to continue the regular routine of twice-weekly weighings, to make sure I was maintaining my eight stones plus, and at Pam's suggestion, (having already discussed the fact that my recuperation period with them was likely to be a little longer than a couple of weeks), registered as a temporary patient at their doctor's surgery.

This latter decision proved to be of enormous value. Firstly I felt that if I had my weight checked officially on a regular basis, then perhaps I could start allowing myself to believe; to stop feeling that maybe all this (life without anorexia/bulimia) was just a dream and that I was kidding myself. Secondly, going to the surgery and meeting Dr Stephen Kidman as an 'ordinary' patient, not an anorectic, helped me further discover what being normal was about. Dr Kidman considered me none other than normal, which at first was quite terrifying. I was so used to visiting a doctor as an unwell person, showing all my weaknesses, and generally coming away clutching a prescription. Meeting a doctor who, even when I cried or showed negative thoughts and feelings, told me I was just being normal, was a real eye-opener, gob-smacker and a wonderful challenge. I could no longer hang on to the excuse of being unwell. I had no excuse any longer – for my thoughts, actions or feelings – except that I was me, and Dr Kidman, on almost every visit, because of his attitude, helped me find my strengths. He believed me, he believed in me, Pam and Ron believed in me. *I* was the Doubting Thomas. I could wallow under the weight of this hat if I wished, but of my own doing I would be thus setting up a rod for my own back. I realised that on my very first visit to Dr Kidman's surgery, and I will never forget that consultation, nor my feelings afterwards and during.

Dr Kidman very kindly agreed to accept me as a temporary patient for whatever length of time necessary, (in the event I stayed in Bournemouth two and a half months). After hearing my history in an introductory consultation he agreed to help me in any way I wished. Hence, we arranged twice weekly weighings, on a Monday and Thursday, at 12.10 p.m. Neither he nor I at this stage realised just how much of a help I was going to be to him too in understanding a little more about the world of eating disorders, but, as this became evident, so I became more motivated to progress quite rapidly. During that first consultation we also discussed possible ways of helping me mobilise and ease my pain. I had already decided that the voiced possibilities of time or life in a wheelchair were not for me! Not yet, anyway! So Doctor Kidman suggested hydrotherapy – three times a week. My instant reaction to that suggestion was, 'No, I can't.' And it was like a reflex action, the reason for which even I didn't know until the doctor asked me. I told him I couldn't possibly wear a swimming costume, but, without giving me more time for thought or justification he replied with the so simple sentence, 'Why not? You are not anorexic now, you have just told me you are recovered, so why is this a problem?'

I couldn't answer. He was right! I had no reason! I was well, even though my new shape and size were still very new and strange to me. I WASN'T ILL ANY MORE. I didn't have anorexia nervosa now.

I didn't commit myself to the hydrotherapy sessions during that consultation, because I felt my boat had been rocked again and I was full of self-doubt. Perhaps anorexia wasn't behind me after all. I was only just considering wearing a bra and trying to get used to my breasts, so perhaps showing it all off, albeit covered by a bathing costume, was too big a step. I reasoned this out with Pam and she seemed sympathetic and understanding regarding

100

what I felt were my limitations. However, she did suggest going into town the next day to buy a bra. At least another step forwards. At that point I decided to go the whole hog or nothing at all. After all 'you have recovered', I told myself. In secret, I decided to accept the hydrotherapy sessions and the next morning, when Pam, her mother and I went into Boscombe, which coincided with them having a dental appointment, and so having to leave me whilst they saw the dentist and hygienist, I slipped off to an underwear and sports shop.

I had no idea what size I was, and so took various sizes into the changing rooms, to emerge eventually with three bras size 34B and a size 12 swimming costume. Pam met me where they had left me, knowing none of all this, and suggested we have a cup of coffee first. The coffee was good and strong, but I couldn't hold back any more, and my tears of relief and achievement started diluting it! I showed Pam and 'Grannie' my purchases and they were full of praise. I for my part, was shocked and pleased at what I had achieved, but also aware that, again, I was actually grieving my anorexia. Into those changing rooms I had also taken clothing measuring a size 28 and 30 chest, knowing they couldn't possibly fit, but feeling I needed to touch them again. Perhaps to see how painfully small I had been and for a few moments to wish I was the same size again – I felt so huge, and looked it now. I told Pam of this and we immediately played the 'glad game'. In this instance our reason to be glad was that the garments I had bought were all sale bargains, and I had saved a considerable amount of money! My three bras I had bought for the price of just one of the smaller size and my swimming costume had cost me half the price of the smaller sizes!! I thus started laughing – bargains still give me a thrill today – and we bought another coffee before driving home – to phone the surgery to confirm my acceptance of the hydrotherapy, and to start wearing what I had bought!

Wearing what I had bought was both funny and painful. For example, I couldn't face wearing a bra all day, so I decided to practise every Sunday for two hours. I vividly recall one Sunday when there was still an hour to go; I felt *awful*, started channelling this emotion into feeling fat and cried and cried when the two hours were up and I took it off to have a bath. Funnily enough, it was that same Sunday that Pam had been quietly envying my figure. (This she told me much later on when I confessed to her how I had been feeling all day).

November saw some very warm weather, and my inbuilt thermostat, being so used to keeping a four stone body warm, instead of eight stones plus, went totally haywire. Hence I was constantly feeling overly hot, and a shirt or blouse was all I needed, no jumpers or cardigans. Most days I had 'suffered' wearing a cardigan or jumper as well, to conceal my shape, but on one particular Sunday, (things always seemed to happen on a Sunday, contrary to the popular song *Never on a Sunday!*), it was just too much. I was wearing trousers and a very pretty blouse, which I had tucked into my waist-band, and I just didn't dare move out of my armchair, despite, longing to go to the loo for several hours! Eventually, of course, I did – it was also remove-bra-go-to-the-loo-and-have-a-bath time, and it was as I made that move that Pam had envied my waistline. I was aghast when she told me, but determined at the same time to face up to wearing all my tops tucked into my waistbands, without anything over them all the time. And I did. Another milestone.

Putting on my swimming costume was a totally different kettle of fish. Having once purchased it, I'm afraid I hid it away in a drawer. After all I wouldn't be needing it until my first hydrotherapy session. However, as that session drew nearer, it occurred to me – and to Pam, of course, – that if I didn't wear it a little bit beforehand, if only to get used to revealing so much of myself, that day might not only prove too horrendous, but impossible too. So, the practice sessions started! Every evening when I got ready for bed, and joined Pam and Ron for an hour or so for supper, I wore it under my dressing gown. Ron constantly tried pulling my leg about his X-ray eyes, as a gentle form of encouragement, I suppose, to shed the robe which I did manage on a couple of occasions. We were all watching the 10.00 p.m. news, with me dressed as if on the sun-drenched Balearic islands. Pam and Ron were in their usual winter fare, and, my goodness was the television our focal point! Not an eye moved, nor a head turned; even Smokey, the cat, watched the television! Our gaze was fixed on that wonderful piece of modern technology, even through the advertisements, and to all and sundry never had the news been so interesting! At 10.30 p.m., I grabbed my dressing gown, shot into my bedroom, removed the swimwear, leapt into my nightie, and dived into bed!

Then came the evening I practised getting it wet – Ron's suggestion again – I had a bath in it! All very well until I realised how much it clung when wet! I was terrified as I caught a sideways glance of myself in the bathroom mirror. I felt enormous, fat, ugly and gross. Through my tears, as I stared at my reflection, I saw only a pathetic being once again – and I hated it. Then I realised slowly and painstakingly, as I remained hidden in the bathroom, until my eyes were less red, that that was what I *felt*, not what I was. I *felt* fat but I wasn't – I knew I was quite slim. 'Felt' was the operative word. I had to substitute another word for fat, find the emotions from which I was once again trying to distract myself, and I thus gradually traced the trigger of my feelings to fear. I was missing the regular routine therapies the hospital had offered, missing, too, being able to express myself to someone who seemed to understand, and was instead now floundering in a sea of self-doubt as to whether I really could make this journey of discovery. Fearful, too.

My diary and logbook received entries every day, by the score, as new feelings, experiences and fears arose, and I therefore got to know myself more and more, as did everyone else. I relied heavily on my written thoughts – perhaps a little too heavily – as I did on keeping my weight *absolutely* right, and I know Pam and Ron would say I was overly rigid in my disciplines, and rather inflexible. However, all I can say to justify those early days is that I was deadly serious and earnest in my wish to make my medical record history, and several excerpts from my logbook show this:

> 'Struggled a little bit this afternoon – enjoying for enjoyment's sake is hard – without having to achieve. Yet I can see that doing this would be an achievement in itself.'
>
> (28/10/90)

> 'A bit of a fat day. Had to persevere with the right quantity of milk, (1/3rd of a pint), at breakfast time; it would have been so easy to cut out, or down. But then why bother? Just what sort of sense of control would this really give me? I know the trigger this time – it was self-doubt again – my very worst enemy. Self-doubt MUST be turned into SELF-ESTEEM.'
>
> (2/11/90)

> 'Cut down on the breakfast milk today. Spent part of the day in tears, so visited Dr Kidman in the evening, although able to present him with a self diagnosis. Cutting back, ie, depriving myself, is an effort to negate all the good things that are going on, as well as what I am achieving, because I don't know how to handle the good ... I feel positive in presenting that self diagnosis, about getting to grips with this.'
>
> (13/11/90)

> 'Have been cooking many of the evening meals now ... Shopping for large amounts of food ... no problem. I'll get there! Felt restless this evening because I was, I think, perhaps hungry. Yet I don't know, I don't recognise this sensation of hunger, so am I really hungry, do I really want/need more, or is it a distraction from an emotion? Is anorexia/bulimia nervosa still hanging around?'
>
> (20/11/90)

'My weight has dropped ½ LB. Clearly that was a hunger message the other day! I have to believe in myself, that such calls/sensations, are simple physical needs. They are not the empty void needing filling, nor emotions welling up that need stuffing back down again. Quite simply, I was hungry. I'M NORMAL!!'

(22/11/90)

'Have found myself feeling inadequate recently, particularly in relation to Grannie's (Pam's mother), *death, and Pam and Ron's distress.* (Grannie had lived in the same building as us, but was very self-sufficient in the 'Grannie-flat'). *Have stopped cutting on the milk, or taking anything out on the food, but unwittingly have over-stretched myself exercise-wise. My legs and hips hurt so much. I can see what I've done – in order to lessen the mental anguish about feeling inadequate, I've caused much more physical pain, so that all my thoughts are focused on that. I'm bloody stupid! I do wish I could catch myself <u>beforehand</u>, instead of in retrospect.'*

(29/11/90)

Having practised wearing my bathing-costume both dry and wet now, I felt in pretty good nick about my first hydrotherapy appointment. Pretty pleased with myself, too, convincing myself constantly that the sessions would not be a problem in terms of body-weight, shape and size. All this had worked well, until I met my hydrotherapist – a man. If I'd had legs that were in running order, no-one would have seen me for dust! For some reason, possibly because all the physiotherapists I'd seen during my stay in the clinic were female, I'd assumed this instructor would also be a lady. So – and what a *so*! – here I was – having been shown to my changing cubicle by a female attendant, standing in my bathing costume, shaking hands, (and knees and everything else), with John, who was very literally a tall dark handsome

105

young man! I was trembling! I don't know exactly why. Obviously I was conscious of my figure, and conscious too, to a degree, of what others might think, but whatever, I blushed, flushed, stammered, stuttered – and, yes, started crying! The latter was probably the best thing I did because it enabled me to be quite open with John about my history and my current anxieties. he took all these on board with only a minimal amount of understanding, but showed a great deal of care, empathy and tenderness, and our relationship was far more valuable than just helping to increase my pain tolerance and muscle power. I had to get used to him holding me, around the waist, across my chest, around my tummy, wherever, as he mobilised my limbs and encouraged me to try and control my own movements. It was yet another way of me accepting and getting used to my shape – and in the event, feeling quite proud of it and liking myself both physically and mentally. Not a way perhaps that I would have chosen, nor recommended, but what, for me, was the very best thing that could have happened. Here was a normal person, treating me as a normal person, and who also addressed the subject of my shape when I felt anxious about it. I'd never had any hang-ups about men, but I think the fact that John was a man did have an added value. He was able to reflect a normal male attitude, without any sexual overtones or innuendos, and he accepted all of me a hundred per cent.

There were days when we laughed and laughed as I tried hopelessly to increase my exercise periods, and there were other days when he threatened me with eviction because my tears were diluting the chlorine balance of the pool! Self-esteem and self-doubt seemed to ping-pong around through the smiles and the tears, but through it all I became a stronger person – both physically and mentally.

Every day during my convalescence in Bournemouth was a special one, marking further progress, as I made my journey of discovery. Some days, of course, stand out more than others, if only because one of my main objectives was to try and help other people understand about eating disorders. Sufferers and non-sufferers alike. During the latter years of my illness, having not been able to, nor been allowed to, die, I had vowed that if I ever came through it, I would do my best to 'tell the world' about the hell of anorexia/bulimia nervosa, and compulsive eating, and try to help others recover too. Tell them what recovery meant, not simply control over eating, but control over expression of feelings and emotions. Hence Pam and Ron's kitchen became my office as I wrote over forty letters to different people and to voluntary help organisations.

I was astonished and disgusted at many of the replies, one, for example, saying they could offer no help because they didn't deal with eating disorders. 'Exactly so', I thought, 'that's why I flipping well wrote to you, to prove the need for help in this area,' and so back I would write. Some of the letters were very encouraging and it became obvious, by mid-December, that I had a lot of support for the 'work' I wanted to do when I returned to my Brighton flat. I wanted to run a help-line from home, and initiate a self-help group for sufferers, with a support one, if needs be, for relatives and friends of sufferers. I was aware, though, that my own personal journey had only recently begun and that over-loading myself might tire me therefore causing me further hardship in my own recovery process. For one, I didn't know if I could face Brighton, and return to a flat that I'd left, in a shitty condition, literally, (vomit and diarrhoea stains were everywhere – I'd too often been too weak to get to the toilet in time), or live on my own, fending for myself, continuing to be my own friend instead of an enemy. Further, I had to consider a whole wardrobe of clothes, all children's sizes, that would have to be discarded, and there were also very many memories to face. On top of that, being so disabled was also difficult and was going to be far harder on my own. Although I do now drive a little, then I couldn't; it was too painful. So shopping and getting out, as well as the normal household chores were all possible problems, solved eventually with the help of the social services, and by applying for mobility and attendance allowances as well as income support and invalidity benefit. This, of course, encompassed other problems. For example, would my income cover my mortgage and bills, as well as food and other necessary items? So I had to work my finances out to the nth degree and think hard, looking at both the pros and cons, about the feasibility or otherwise of actually returning to Brighton at all. Discovering that I could just manage financially, using a three-week menu cycle, hence buying more in bulk and making good use of my fridge-freezer, I decided I had to find out if I could manage emotionally and asked Pam and Ron if they would come with me for a visit. We decided to make a day-trip on 7th November, 1990.

That day was very difficult, but successful. I knew, as did Pam think, that I'd either put the key in the lock and not be able to step over the threshold, or indeed step over and face it. Strangely enough, the latter was not a difficult thing to do, but yes, I did cry, and quite a lot – sorting out my wardrobe, for example. I'd been sure that some things would fit, but there was nothing except for the big baggy jumpers in which I had latterly tried to disguise myself. My feet were two sizes larger, and a 'B' fitting instead of 'AA', so we found four dustbin liners, two for putting clothes to throw, one for giving to charity, and one for washing and dry-cleaning, with a view to possible fitting alterations being made. Apart from two baggy jumpers, I was left with just three items. Knickers and underwear, as well as night attire, had all had to go, too, as well as all my outdoor coats and jackets, – it was hard – and scary – to realise just how thin I had been. Pam and Ron were a marvellous support that day; without them I know I could not have managed, and would have probably decided I couldn't cope with Brighton. After all, one option we had all considered was of me living in Bournemouth, so that if I needed help, support or encouragement, it would be there. Facing the bathroom and the kitchen was like a nightmare, and memories flooded back. The vomit and shit stains on the carpet walls and furniture throughout the flat had to be cleaned off and I found it too distressing. Pam and Ron knuckled under, scrubbing every-thing in sight, and in the end the place was almost shining (although at a later stage I did have to re-new my carpets). We decided that anything that held ghastly memories was best discarded, and out went a lot of kitchenware.

I recall Ron being rather puzzled when I insisted that a set of saucepans be thrown out. To him, they looked quite good, 'especially', he said, 'with a bit of a clean'. My head down, and crying some more, my face turned a brilliant shade of red as I told him I'd used those saucepans, as I had many containers and utensils, for vomiting and going to the toilet, because both bodily functions often came without warning, not, as I've said, giving me time – and I didn't have the energy, either – to get to the bathroom. Without more ado we became ruthless. No questions needed to be asked. What had to go, went, Pam and Ron stressing they did not feel at all disgusted at, or ashamed of, me. As a consequence of all this I was left with very little – but enough.

Although that day was upsetting, we did laugh too, and we had to. My history was a horror story but a real one, and the state of the flat epitomised that. To 'allow' my bingeing to continue disguised as I said initially, with the attitude just in case I had any visitors, I'd always kept in the house and in fact hoarded, a lot of foodstuffs. These particular ones I now speak of though not being of the instant variety that I could stuff from a can or packet, or the fridge or freezer, but of the baking sort such as flour, sugar and pasta (for those visitors who came to dinner!), and it was the latter, the pasta that caused us to laugh. I had jars and jars of it – all very high smelling and, as it turned out, most over five years old! The mould that had developed on all the different shapes actually looked quite pretty, but, oh! the pong on removing the lids! The greatest shame was in having to throw away the jars – now quite expensive and collectable – whilst the pasta refused to come out. The jars inverted, it still stuck to the base and it resisted, too, all attempts we had with a hammer and chisel!! Overcome by the smell, and with laughing, we had to give in and throw it all away. As Ron said, 'There's white pasta, red pasta, green pasta, brown pasta, and whole-meal pasta, but BLUE, Ann, – no way!'

As a result of that day-return to Brighton, I knew for sure that I wanted to go back there to live and was hell-bent on getting on with my recovery to do just that. I therefore became more positive, setting new goals. I frequented most of the local charity shops in order to establish a new wardrobe, on my income. (I had also received the maximum allowance of £150.00 for just this purpose from the DHSS, a special discretionary payment), and started doing more of the big household shopping. The actual spending of £50.00 in one spree on a trolleyfull of food *for me* alone, though, almost made me faint the first time; *I* was going to eat all this? I felt a fat greedy pig immediately, even though I knew I wouldn't be eating it in the old (bulimic) way, nor all at once. I knew that it represented two months' food, all bar the fresh produce, but it made me feel so shaky to think that in the old days, I'd thought nothing of a £50 spend-out on one single binge; those days when I ate everything in sight, as if there was no tomorrow. Dear Ron had to accompany me out of the superstore on that first occasion, and pretty quickly too. He kept telling not to worry, but aware of my anxiety level, suggested that perhaps I ought to get into the trolley too, making heading for the car a little easier for all of us – the trolley having a mind of its own; suddenly though, it all seemed quite funny, Ron attempting to push the trolley and hold my arm at the same time, me in a complete daze, and once again we were soon laughing, Ron teasing me about whether I'd bought enough heavy puds!

My hair, having now fully regrown, was surprisingly quite a gleaming crown of glory – amazing just what one of the good things a sound nutritional diet can do – but it was in need of a cut. During my illness I had hated visits to the hairdresser's; my face being so gaunt and hollow made any framing of my face difficult. As the stylist snipped away, so the scissor blades would disappear into an eye socket, or just below my very prominent cheek bones. I dreaded a visit now, not for the same reason, of course, but because mirrors and acknowledging my new physical shape were still difficult, even though I refer in this instance, only to my face. However, it was during a wander round one of the big stores in Bournemouth, that a beautician picked me out amongst all the shoppers and asked me if I would be a make-up model for her 3.00 p.m. display, that I began to think differently. The beautician said she had asked me because of my fine features and good skin! Although I did refuse at first, her persistence led me to the chair, and there I underwent a free make-up, to the admiration of many on-lookers, and for me, a mixture of bewilderment, embarrassment and pleasure. At the end I was asked to look in the mirror to see what I thought. I felt I wanted to run off, but obliged, and was astonished, that I managed to look at myself in public, and that the reflection staring back was really OK.

'Now,' I thought obviously somewhat uplifted, 'is the time for a haircut' and immediately went into a hairdresser's requiring models – so I would pay less – and booked low-lights, with a cut and blow dry for the following day. Again I went home in a daze. Had I done the right thing? Talk about 'in for a penny in for a pound'! Why hadn't I just booked a cut and blow dry so I wouldn't have to sit in front of a mirror for so long? As it was this appointment was going to be three hours! Still – I guess that's me. I looked upon it as a challenge and went home to tell Pam and Ron of my intentions, and as I stepped into the house Ron let out a wolf-whistle. 'You look lovely', he said, 'it's the first time I've seen you wearing any make-up, and it really suits you. Why don't you wear a little every day?'

I determined there and then to do just that. I figured spending a little extra time in front of the mirror every day, if only to apply mascara, and a little blusher, would help me further to accept my new shape as well as help me to indulge myself. And it did.

The day of the hairdresser's appointment also apparently marked the day Pam and Ron felt I had 'made it'. They have often referred to it since as the day I finally showed I could laugh at myself; that the all too serious Ann was relaxing more. I had no idea what my flippant remark to them, as I left the house, signified. Quite simply I had made a joke about having my hair done by a junior stylist: 'If I'm not home for tea, you'll know the colour went wrong and I've gone bright orange. At least if I become a missing person, it will be easy for the police to spot me.'

I left as nervous as ever I can remember, and Pam and Ron – well I think they had a snooze! – more confident still in me, and satisfied I was well on the way. The appointment went well and I was very pleased with the result. However, my nervousness drained me completely and by the end of the three hours I was becoming tearful. Ron came to collect me, not having recognised me at first. 'I was looking for someone with bright orange hair' he said. And again I was suddenly laughing.

The rate at which I showed improvement – physically, emotionally and socially – was noted by everyone, and, in fact, was astonishing everyone, as well as me. Paul Renyard, the vicar of St Barnabas Church in Bournemouth, (Pam and Ron's church, where I subsequently married), recently told me that as I started climbing my mountains, so both he and the congregation had at first watched, waiting to catch me when I fell, then when it was plain that I was climbing up quite steadily, started climbing with me. I've often thought about that remark. What wonderful friends I have, but little did they know the weak emotional side of me then that I kept hidden. Progressing so well was proving difficult to accept.

'I slipped up today after such a long period of success. I have just felt totally unable to acknowledge my achievements gracefully, ie; shopping, (food and clothes), cooking, eating well and maintaining my weight, socialising, attending hydrotherapy, wearing my shirts tucked in belted-at-the-waist clothes, buying and wearing a swimming costume, and bras, and other feminine clothes, and products, having my hair cut and using make-up. These things

112

*to celebrate I have had to be quiet about because to
everyone else they are normal, so I've stolen six
postcards. I couldn't resist the drive/compulsion. I
gave in to the inner conflict. I refuse to do it again:
there is no need to degrade or hate myself any more.
Nor is there any reason. I must share what I achieve
more, and what I'm having difficulty with, even if it's
just with you,* (my logbook)'.

(Logbook entry 19/11/90)

As December and Christmas were approaching, and after
another day-return to Brighton, I planned that I would
spend the fortnight before Christmas back in my flat, to see
if I could manage on my own. I was going to return to
Bournemouth for the festive period itself and then reflect
further as to my future. Pam and Ron, meanwhile, decided
to go and spend the New Year and the following six weeks
in the USA, with their daughter, her husband and their
recently born grandson. They felt that should any crisis
occur on my part, my new-found friends in Bournemouth
would rally round, and I think too, they also knew I would
manage. They gave me complete freedom of their house,
and, in fact, everything they had, but most of all their trust.
However, there were two rather large hiccups before their
departure, which made me almost crumble with self-doubt,
and which also caused Pam some concern, particularly 30th
November.

30th November, 1990, was a Friday – hydrotherapy day
and fish and chip night. Whilst in the swimming pool, I had
not felt at all well, and had channelled all my energies, yet
again, into feelings of fatness and self-repugnance. I said
nothing about it upon returning home, and in fact said
nothing at all – because I was so convinced anorexia nervosa
was still a part of me – causing Pam to ask me if I was all
right. I told her I was fine, (meaning anything but, of
course), but when it came to Ron popping out to the chippy,
I asked if they would mind if I didn't eat with them.

I'd eat a little later. They agreed to this, and tucked into their usual at about 6.30 p.m., popping mine into the oven to keep warm. I, meanwhile, was aware that I didn't want anything to eat. For the first time in so many months, I just did not want to eat a meal. I was tormenting myself with thoughts of anorexia. Obviously I didn't want to eat because I was still ill and wanted to lose weight! At about 8.00 p.m. Pam asked me how long it was going to be before I had dinner, and I replied, 'In a few minutes'. At 8.30 p.m. she asked the same question and I gave the same reply. At 9.00 p.m. she got up, switched off the television, (a convenient source of distraction), came over to my chair and told me if I didn't tell her what the matter was, she'd call out the doctor immediately. I let go my fear and terror in a flood of tears, shouting, 'I'm still ill, I don't want to eat. For the first time for so long I just don't want a meal. Obviously I'm still ill".

Pam put her arm round me and asked me to try and tell her why I didn't want to eat. I said I'd been feeling a bit nauseous most of the day, but was scared it was anorexia. Pam refused to even contemplate that possibility, 'feeling off-colour is quite normal', she said, 'and so is going to bed early if you don't feel well,' at the same time packing me off to my bedroom, suggesting I leave my meal this time.

Funnily enough, having identified how I felt, ie, nausea, rather than irrational fear alone, the relief was so great, I decided to try to eat something and Pam mashed up some of the fish into some potatoes, giving me a yoghurt to follow. This however, made me feel more nauseous than ever. I knew I was going to be sick, and terrifying visions of the old head-hanging-over-the-toilet days flooded back. I'd failed, I wasn't going to recover, and I went to the bathroom. Up came what I had eaten, along with an attack of diarrhoea – and some blood. It was 1.00 a.m. 1st December. I had started my first period for more than twenty two years. I was normal after all! I *had* been feeling nauseous! I *had* been feeling unwell! I *was* off-colour! This wasn't anorexia!

114

> *'What a way to begin a month. A period! My first for 22 years or more! Perhaps that's why there has been so much self-doubt around this last week, and why I've been feeling down and depressed. I'm normal! It's just P.M.T.! It's great! I don't mind feeling a bit off-colour. I'm really a woman and I'm beginning to feel quite proud. I could become a mother! I wonder if I'll ever be a wife'.*
>
> (Logbook entry 1/12/90)

Following log book entries began to show more self-assuredness:

> *'I'm so lucky to be alive! ... I belong to the community – to Brighton and to Bournemouth. I have a right to live ... at long last I have a sense of belonging and feel love abounds, and, free now, I can receive it and give back in return. Fantastic!'*
>
> (Logbook entry 4/12/90)

My return to Brighton, from 7th December – 22nd December also reflected this self-assuredness, and proved to be a successful venture. Even though I knew I would be returning, leaving Pam and Ron was still a wrench, and I cried on our parting, sensing the floundering feelings again, and the self-doubt. I discovered, however, during those two weeks that I *had* got my own strengths, and personality, that I *could* meet new people and share time with others, *of my own accord*. I realised, thankfully, that I could manage without Pam and Ron, and I think, that was the best bonus of all for us. I had thought that without them I would fall over; they were my props and my crutches, I was weak. Instead I discovered I was quite strong; that although Pam and Ron provided support it did not mean I depended on them. Support meant *interdependence* and it had helped me become more competent. Being the Doubting Thomas as ever, though, always on the look out for pitfalls that might cause me to return to coping with life through food and

115

body abuse, I was aware that perhaps the only reason for coping so well in Brighton was that I knew I was going to return to Bournemouth, so once again I didn't allow myself to experience, fully, all my achievements, nor give myself a pat on the back. Also Christmas was now fast approaching; a festive season which I had never before really celebrated. I wasn't frightened of the abundance of food, but rather my inability to, and lack of knowledge in, 'letting go' and enjoying myself. I didn't realise either that three weeks had gone by since that first hiccup, and that the self-doubts and fears were establishing a familiar, (although as far as my naivety was concerned, an unfamiliar) pattern.

Christmas itself was a wonderful occasion. We went the whole hog with Christmas decorations, a tree, and the traditional turkey and pud, plus extra trimmings, along with, of course, a Christmas cake and mince pies. I was astounded to receive over sixty cards, and so very many presents. As it was a real first for me, I was easily overwhelmed, and 10.00 a.m. on Christmas morning saw me sitting in the armchair, tears pouring down my cheeks as I looked at all my cards and beautifully wrapped gifts. I simply didn't feel deserving of all this. As a family we spent the rest of the day entertaining ourselves, having decided the television was taboo, and thus indulged in lots of fun and games, although again I was aware of the need to cut down on my fun, because of feeling I didn't deserve so much enjoyment. The cutting-down urge manifested itself at the table with the need to cut down/out on some of the trimmings. I didn't after all, require sage and onion stuffing, roast potatoes, boiled potatoes, pureed carrots and parsnips and sprouts as well as the turkey and sausages, I told myself. However, a little question came into my head: 'Why not? Why not have a go?'. So I did! It was all very lovely and I slowly let the guilt, ie; the non-deserving feeling go away. After all, living is not based on a system of rewards and punishments, shoulds and should-nots, and this is something I uphold today, and something that goes very much against the grain of my upbringing. (My parents considered family attitudes and love, for example, to be a

116

duty, duties being met reaping rewards. I disagree with this in that I do not consider family relationships should be based on duty, for me they are about mutual respect and friendship, which will then quite probably encompass love).

On Boxing Day, we had another pleasant and quiet day together, Pam and Ron getting ready for their departure to the States on the 28th, but I was very tearful. I put it down to anxieties surrounding their going away, and indeed likewise on the 27th and 28th, but things seemed even worse on the 27th when I discovered I had lost half a pound in weight. I was ill again! Anorexia was back! I was not going to be able to cope on my own! I might never see Pam and Ron again! In my desperate panic I made an appointment to see Dr Kidman the next evening – a Friday-fish-and-chip-night in which I would probably never be able to indulge again! Invitations were also coming left, right and centre from friends in Bournemouth to join them for lunches, dinners, and New Year festivities. I couldn't face any of them. I felt a loser, and I was losing fast.

The consultation on the Friday evening with Dr Kidman, as it happened, provided me with a real, but positive shock. I remember tearfully confessing to the doctor, showing him all the negative thoughts and feelings I had written in my logbook, that I was anorexic again. He, though, quite calmly, but firmly and wholeheartedly disagreeing with me, replied, 'you are not anorexic, you are pre-menstrual!' I gaped at him. Me! No! I couldn't be, and in my disbelief I asked how did he know, how could he be sure! The answer to that, of course, was that the proof would involve just waiting – and seeing. Meanwhile I could choose to disbelieve him, not go visit any of my friends, and remain feeling very sad and negative. I decided I'd have to try and believe him and made a very real effort when I got home, to phone all those people who had extended an arm of hospitality and accept their invitations. I also invited some friends to come visit me, and thus committed myself to something every day for the next ten days. I felt washed out and exhausted after all that, but brought the evening to a close with a bath – and yes, fish and chips! I went to bed tired and tearful again and kept the radio on for comfort throughout the night in the hope that my awful self-doubt and fears would disperse. They did, but not until two days had passed.

> *'Another period! One day late. It's incredible to be so clockwork after all these years. Had to cry and laugh all in one go! Cry with sheer pleasure and wonder, and laugh, because despite having been told by Dr Kidman two days ago that my tears and self-doubt were probably nothing else other than PMT it still didn't occur to me to be prepared. Tampons have never been on my shopping list! Had to phone up Liz from church to help me out. I literally was caught with my trousers down – at 2.00 p.m. today! I guess I'm finding it hard to believe it could really happen to me, that I could/can be so normal. Almost perfect! Anorexia Nervosa isn't around, only Ann Cox! This journey of discovery is absolutely fascinating. OK, I cry sometimes, but I've learned now the importance of, and ability to, hang on to my feelings. Experience feelings is the true essence. I cannot solve anything'.*

(Logbook entry 30/12/90)

I wasn't the only one to be both delighted and relieved that this hiccup was just that and nothing more. Pam was equally so. She and Ron now in the States, she telephoned that Sunday, giving me her news and asking me for mine, and upon hearing about my second period, gave three cheers down the telephone. She, too, had been concerned about my tearfulness before they left, and obvious down-heartedness, and had herself experienced doubts – about their departure. She had prayed she and Ron had not decided upon the wrong thing, and my news confirmed their choice to be right.

118

Being normal with regard to menstruation wasn't the only surprise I had, nor pleasure. Going to the toilet was of great concern to me. I didn't want a lifetime of enemas, and I certainly wasn't *ever* going to take laxatives again, but would my body start working again properly, all by itself after so much purgative abuse? If I 'didn't go' for a couple of days I used to become quite panicky – perhaps I'd never function properly? The early days with regard to this issue were very frightening, but I found talking about it and writing about it to be of great help. Without being obsessive about my diet, I ate healthily, including, on a daily basis, wholemeal bread, Weetabix, fresh vegetables (green) and potatoes, and a piece of fruit occasionally. This did not mean I abstained from other foods, including fats, carbohydrates, sugar etc. No food was to be a 'forbidden food' after all – quite simply that daily inclusion was an 'in lieu' of laxatives. And gradually it worked. As time went by I began to establish a fairly regular routine, which now means I usually go every day, and usually first thing in the morning, but not always. I have no fears now, either, with regard to constipation and this lack of worry is usually justified by a visit to the loo later in the day, although I must confess, should I feel overly tired, or there is an abundance of self-doubt, it does niggle me, but not as it did in the latter part of 1990 and the first few months of 1991. Then it was a very, very difficult issue:

'My tummy feels so fat. I haven't been to the loo, I'm scared I'll have to have a lifetime of enemas.'
(Logbook entry 23/10/90)

'I didn't have my full quota of milk at breakfast time. Surely if my stomach doesn't know what to do with all the waste products, I don't need to add to the problem by eating so much?'
(Logbook entry 1/11/90)

'A bit of a fat day today, until 6.00 p.m., when I went to the loo. Such a relief! I really must relax about it. My body can work quite well of its own accord. I mustn't be so anxious about it. There's no need'.

(Logbook entry 2/11/90)

'Feel unclean inside, a bit low and a bit fat. Self-doubt again. Suddenly I feel it all hinges on going to the toilet properly, as it did when I was ill. A good purge and I felt cleansed, albeit temporarily. If only I could go to the loo today, perhaps I'd feel better inside? It's not so much that I want to feel absolutely emptied, or clean exactly, but going to the toilet does have some important connotations for me, although exactly what, I'm not sure. Perhaps it's quite simple, though – the more my bodily functions work normally the more the wheel of confidence turns, to becoming self-perpetuating.'

(Logbook entry 25/11/90)

'I'm scared of being weighed tomorrow. I haven't been to the toilet for 4 days and I've continued to eat properly. I must be HUGE.'

(Logbook entry 29/12/90)

(As it turned out I had gained six ounces, and on the following weigh-day, when I had started going to the toilet again on a regular basis, without altering my diet, I had lost a further two ounces! So still my body image was distorted).

'A small amount of fear around, not having gone to the toilet for a couple of days; I've been feeling fat, but I've traced the trigger of that to anxiety about future events, and self-doubt with regard to maintaining my ability to go on acknowledging the past without letting it threaten me any longer.'

(Logbook entry 17/1/91)

120

Discovering that my laxative abuse had far greater, and more devastating *mental* affects than physical was a great shock. Having taken so many laxatives over such a great length of time meant they had become a very real psychological crutch. I had seen them in both as a cleansing and punishing thing, and when I stopped taking them, I was initially afraid of normal bowel actions and of constipation, this becoming yet another problem area to overcome. I also suffered mental anguish from the dreadful physical symptoms – for example the oedema whilst I was in the clinic, and the feeling of fatness as expressed in some of the above exerts from my logbook, along with distorted images of huge amounts of weight gain. I kept having to remind myself that most medical evidence suggests that laxatives *do not* aid weight loss. Any apparent weight loss shown is only temporary, because it is not body tissue lost, but the body suffering dehydration. It is fluids and valuable vitamins and minerals that are lost, rather than calories. Constantly trying to think in this way helped me to persevere, as did talking and writing, Pollyanna, Winnie-the-Pooh, and my sheer bloody-minded determination to meet anything challenging head on, and win.

Thinking, talking and writing as I continued to do helped climbing my mountains greatly, to the extent that sometimes I seemed to shin up the sides at an alarming rate, rather than the more gradual process I and everybody else had expected; ie a gentle climb with many a slip backwards. Of course, as can be seen by the excerpts from my logbook and diaries, nothing was easy, nor was it straightforward, and when self-doubt ruled over self-esteem, I did indeed slip backwards, but not as much, perhaps, as I might have done. I realised that the anorectic patterns of thought – a habit of so many years – couldn't possibly disappear overnight. The difference lay in recognising them, understanding the trigger, and not acting upon them. Having thought thus far, I was determined then to see any slip-up as only natural and *normal*, not a failure. In the early days I was not always able to apply this objective attitude, but on the whole I did. Any slip I tried to turn into a constructive learning experience, as I was intent on doing with regard to my years of hell. I had to pass on my knowledge and understanding to others.

Learning to differentiate between a slip and a failure was very difficult, perhaps, more so, because most of my life I had seen myself as a rejected failure, and also regarding exams etc, I had never failed anything. In some ways, I wish I had failed an exam or two because I feel failure, ie, not being perfect, is something we should all learn to accept gracefully as a part of living. I love Rudyard Kipling's poem *If*, and I think many lines in his verse are poignant – particularly with regard to meeting Triumph and Disaster, Success and Failure just the same. Once again, playing Pollyanna's glad game, and finding the good in the bad came in very useful in helping the self-perpetuating wheel of self-confidence, self-esteem and self-respect turn, and I began to realise that I did indeed have an identity without food and bodily abuse. I could be, and was, a somebody after all:

> *I am Me*
> *And you are you.*
> *And together we live on this planet.*
> *If I were you,*
> *And you were me*
> *My name might even be Janet.*
> *But I am Ann*
> *And you? you're you,*
> *And I wouldn't give me up for a minute.*
> *I'm special, I'm free,*
> *And you're special, too,*
> *But I like me too much to redeem it.*
>
> (Diary entry 11/1/91)

One of the things I also did in order to keep seeing things in a positive light, was to write out a list of self-indulgences, to which I could refer in a down moment. Allowing myself to enjoy things for my sake alone was totally new, but an important thing to be able to do. For one, it helped me experience the feelings of pleasure, and secondly, it provided me time in my own space, to feel worthy of some self-spoiling, and to relax. Such indulgences included a bubble-bath, a manicure, (home style), reading a magazine or book, watching television, listening to the radio, and, of late, since marrying, baking and sewing, and gardening, each of which I find immensely therapeutic, perhaps because I am then using my creative abilities – regarding the first two, anyway. Writing that list of self-indulgences initially was very very difficult indeed. It seemed like too much ice cream, and was just as difficult as most people find it to be when asked to write down all that they like about themselves and dislike about themselves. (Generally speaking the latter well outweighs the former.)

I sometimes think we are a nation brought up only to complain and to criticise, rather than praise, and that, regarding both ourselves and others. How easy it is to think, yet not say, how nice somebody looks, and how easy to look at what we haven't done instead of at what we have done. Hence, perhaps, the pressures within society currently, to always be striving to achieve. Thankfully I have been able to stop doing that now. Yes, I have goals, and even dreams, but I also wallow in self-satisfaction at times, even if it's only getting all the ironing done – or just smiling at people a few times, and seeing them smile back!

The ten days I have spoken of, after seeing Dr Kidman during that premenstrual time, were great fun and I realised with even more certainty that I did indeed want to help others. I was already coming into contact with many sufferers in Brighton and Bournemouth, (after a little publicity in both local newspapers), and I was still keeping in touch with fellow patients from the clinic, many of whom were giving, or had given-up hope of recovery.

'What a day! Welcomed in the New Year for the first time. Had a meal with the Bourne family, some more new-found friends … Like the line in Cliff Richard's song 'Congratulations,' 'I WANT THE

123

WORLD TO KNOW I'M HAPPY AS CAN BE!"'
(Diary entry 1/1/91)

'Just heard Ken Dodd on the radio; 'Happiness, oh!
happiness, the greatest gift that I possess.' It is too,
but it's not for me alone – others can enjoy it; they
MUST REALISE IT.'
(Diary entry 3/1/91)

I deemed it fit to return to Brighton permanently, (albeit very free and welcome to return to Bournemouth, to stay or visit), on 9th January. With the help of the local Brighton and Hove newspaper and another feature about my recovery, my help-line was due to open up on the 10th, so all the hard work I had done over the last few months was coming to fruition! Also, one particular women's association, in Brighton, called Threshold, was very keen to help me initiate a self-help group for eating disorder sufferers. I was little prepared, though, for what was to come – much publicity, television appearances and radio broadcasts and many many press and magazine interviews, as well as talks around the country, giving me the opportunity to do just what I wrote in my dairy on 1st January – let the world know I was as happy as could be! I survived all this, I'm sure, because of the many preparatory steps I had taken before my return, as well as continuing to write in my logbook and diary. I took the whole thing very seriously indeed, perhaps too seriously, but I knew I was returning to Brighton without any need or cause to feel either isolated or lonely. My mobility and attendance allowances, and invalidity benefit had now been sorted, I had a home-help – a lovely lady – to come in twice a week to do the washing, ironing, cleaning and any shopping or other needs I might have. My twice-weekly weighings were to be continued officially with my Brighton GP Dr Tredgold, and I had regular contact with a social worker, in case I needed any particular help. My disabled orange car badge had come through, and I was going to be retired, possibly with a pension.

On a personal level, I had worked out my three-weekly menu cycle. One, to help me shop well in advance, and two, I wanted to be certain, with regard my eating, that I would never get into the 'what do you fancy tonight' or 'don't feel hungry' routines. Hunger and thirst were still very new sensations to me, and it would have been too easy to go without. Especially when the help-line was very busy. I felt that it might well trigger off the old coping methods of starve and binge when the pressures and self-doubt came. I had also joined a very active church, which had many activities during the week, as well as a Scrabble and Bridge club, and a social club for the physically handicapped and able-bodied, (PHAB). I was determined to make the very most of my new life. My thirty ninth birthday was approaching on 30th January and this I was determined to celebrate by baking, (and eating!) my own birthday cake, putting just one candle in it to celebrate my 're-birth', going out for a meal and just enjoying myself, 'enjoying' being the operative word. Life and living were going to be enjoyable from now on, and I was going to experience it!

Because of the severity of my illness, I was also awarded a place in a day centre, but within a week I knew this *was not* (despite recommendation to the contrary) for me. I did not feel I needed such support, nor the style of therapy on offer and I was disappointed that the initial acceptance of the placement was not going to lead to establishing new friends. Most of the members at the centre were still rather unwell, many on medication and I felt, but perhaps I'm wrong, that they were not motivated to recover, or progress, rather willing to accept their lot, and perhaps avoid any further deterioration. I agonised over my decision not to continue attendance, aware all the time that many things, – life, people etc – were all still new, and maybe a sort of novelty, which was bound to wear off. The niggling questions and doubts in my head came from fears of how I would manage when all the newness had dulled a little, but balanced against the fact that I felt being a day-centre patient might actually hold me back from progressing and reeked too much of psychiatric care and non self-sufficiency, I felt I had to take the plunge and go it alone. I wanted to go on climbing up those mountains! That decision and conclusion was again reached by a good logbook thrashing.

I felt quite strong when I announced my decision. Having faced Choice once again, and dealt with it well, I felt an even greater boost of self-confidence. It seemed that every move, every decision, everything I now did was self-perpetuating in making me feel more confident, and more worthy, hence leading to greater self-esteem. Equally, though, there were pitfalls – especially my tendency to confront myself all the time, and be so self-critical and full of doubt.

> *'I cannot and must not continue to analyse/criticise my every thought and action, because I'll never win, and winning all the time, (ie, getting it right/ perfect) was no doubt a trigger of my illness. Relax Ann! You are OK! You prove it to yourself daily. Be satisfied with that. Nothing you do can really convey your recovery one hundred per cent, nor your love of life, nor your hard-fought, but well-won battle. Time will tell ... Meanwhile, well done! Keep it up, and if you are tearful or a bit low during the next few days, remember that according to the calendar you might be premenstrual! NORMAL!! Yes, that great, wonderful ordinary adjective – NORMAL!!'*
>
> (Logbook entry 15/1/91)

My telephone help-line took off beyond my wildest dreams. I had returned to Brighton to help others in the town because, when I needed it, there was 'nobody there'. I had determined that there was going to be someone there now, – me – and I knew, although I had no real evidence, mainly because of the secrecy behind eating disorders, that there were a lot of unwell people in Brighton. However, I felt it would be absolutely the wrong thing to do to go it alone. A lot of unwell people putting their emotional

126

distress my way could be a burden which I couldn't possibly carry, and anyway, whichever hospital or psychiatric services I had been in, or under, over the years, I had noticed the staff comprised a team. This had appeared occasionally to have drawbacks and frustrated me, considerably sometimes, because there never seemed to be any continuity. Often the staff seemed to be working independently of one another, and without knowing it, in a completely different direction. Nevertheless, I did appreciate the necessity for a team; for one, the important opportunity of off-loading and keeping oneself mentally healthy, and it was with this line of thought that I had written some of those many letters back in Bournemouth, establishing my own team, although 'sleeping' rather than active members. Ready and very keen to back me were my GP, a psychiatric nurse, a community psychiatric nurse, a (new-to-Brighton) eating disorder specialist and a social worker. They all felt 'it would be a pleasure', if only then because in some small, although indirect, way, that was their opportunity to help people suffering eating disorders – their only other way generally being to refer sufferers on.

As it turned out, my 'team' was just that, a support and back-up. I suppose I had viewed them as probable props for when I fell over, but I never did. Knowing they were there if needed seemed to be sufficient most of the time, and I paced myself in answering what turned out initially to be an average of 150 calls a week (it has escalated considerably since then). Pam and Ron gave me one of their old answering machines, which I had serviced, so when needs be I could have a rest, go out, eat a meal, or just sit and be idle, without callers feeling the terrifying despair of 'nobody there'. Callers were free to leave a message (as are they today) and/or telephone number so that I could return their call, as I always did. However, only being able to answer a maximum of fifteen to twenty calls, generally speaking, in one day, I soon had a terrific backlog. But I kept my pace steady. I felt more positive – I had been right, there were a lot of ill people 'hiding' out there – and I did all that I could and to the best of my ability, as indeed I still do. I could, and can, only do my best, and with calls coming from all over the British Isles before long, as well as from abroad now, I have to strictly – and constantly – remind myself of that from time to time.

My attitude was, and is, that with anorexia/bulimia nervosa behind me, as a way of coping with life, the eating disorder was not going to give me a 'backhander' by way of me wearing myself out and wearing myself down in my intent to help others. It was important to keep a clear perspective of my life as *ME*, not as a 'saviour', nor as a workaholic. I realised that very quickly, and tried not to panic as the calls flooded in. I liked me, now, and I wanted and needed to enjoy living and life to the full. I knew too, that with my meagre income, I could not return all the calls even though I was only telephoning back to say that I was now free to speak to whoever and that they could phone in again. But that was not my fault, and I determined not to feel guilty or distressed by this in any way. Further, not always returning the call motivated the caller to phone again which is not as bad as sometimes thought. You see in the business of self-help, one of the steps is asking for help. Telephoning/asking a first time is often easy. A second time less so, and may help prove to the sufferer their tenacity or otherwise. I needed my income support and invalidity benefit, and allowances, for myself, in order to have a reasonable standard of life and it was important to remember this (Fortunately that problem has and is occasionally overcome by the odd few monetary donations through the post).

I feel very privileged and proud to say I succeeded, even though on one particular evening I came home to a message from a distressed mother, whose daughter had just died from bulimia nervosa. She blamed me for her daughter's death, because I had not been available for a chat with Vicky ten days ago. I cried, of course. It was a bad situation, but I could and would not take on board any blame; likewise with distressing calls today. I was, and am human;

thus I had, and have my limitations. I couldn't be there, nor can I be there, all the time to help everyone at the precise time they want the help, and I don't have any magical cures or answers, as I told Vicky's mother. There are none. She seemed to think that had Vicky and I talked to one another her daughter would not have died. I could, and can, only do my best – and I knew I had – and told my logbook and diary just that!

A conclusion to a chapter such as this, entitled 'Journey of Discovery', is really impossible if only because surely that's really what everybody's life is – a learning process, a journey of discovery, and therefore an on-going thing, just as were my fears for a while:

> *'...this journey of discovery certainly has its moments of identity crisis; singing along with the radio one minute, crying the next, especially around PMT time. But I'm NORMAL, and how wonderful to feel free to cry – and to know I can stop crying ... I know I'm strong enough to do none other than continue moving forward, but boy, does self-doubt sometimes get the better of me, and frighten me!'*

(Logbook entry 5/1/91)

On many occasions I likened my journey to that of the long distance runner, not to emphasise so much the loneliness/isolation of it all, but rather the great effort and energy it demands. Also it has been, and will probably always be, the longest journey because it is the journey inwards. It is such a marathon, but having stepped out of the eating disorder prison, I'm free to go anywhere and everywhere, and do anything and everything I want to, now, – providing I *really* want to do it. It is me and my motivation that sets me my goals and ambitions, and they, unless I choose otherwise, are limitless; it is me alone who decides whether to indeed set these challenges and then meet them. No-one can do it for me, (although, of course, they can encourage me), as could no-one other than me, free myself from my anorexia/bulimia. Running, to me, symbolises and symbolised freedom, not simply running into another limited space, and more loneliness. It also gave me a chance to get to know myself, – an entirely new person – a *real* experience – which evoked many fears, anxieties, but also laughter. My long distance running in my journey of discovery gradually became less and less a steep uphill climb; I was no longer heading downhill either, and it eventually began to even out on the flat, to become an endless marathon of wonderment:

> *It's good to be a woman*
> *And to be recognised as just that,*
> *Already sitting down to the banquet*
> *– and eating – with relish – to Enjoy.*
> *My shape is not completely full, and rounded,*
> *– just a little more roundness, with curves is*
>   *needed.*
> *Feminity, slimness, womanhood, and Ann ...*
> *I'm almost there because already my void is almost*
>   *full up*
> *– I'm wanted, needed and loved*
> *And – free – I'm able to give back in return.*
>   (23/1/91)

By the beginning of February, after delivering a public open forum to anyone and everyone interested, in Brighton, and further afield, as it turned out, I had also established a self-help group for sufferers. One I chose not to call mine, but rather theirs because it was *they* who had to learn to identify their feelings and needs, and go beyond the physical manifestations of food, body-weight, shape and size obsessions. I viewed myself only as the conductor, who from my own experiences would occasionally see the need to draw them back from talking about their symptoms, in order to look beyond and try to find the real, (possibly quite deeply buried), EMOTIONS.

Naturally, running a help-line, a self-help group, receiving much publicity, and establishing new friends through the church and various social clubs, all helped to make me feel wanted, and a part of the community and the world, but I was aware, despite, at this stage, having had several dates with various men I had met, that there was still an 'emptiness' of some sort. The sexual desires and feelings I experienced, which were at times quite strong – but then again, quite normal – I kept undercover. I suppose in retrospect, it would have been easy to give into them, but I didn't feel it right, and knew it might leave me feeling very, very vulnerable indeed. I felt they were something from which I might always have to distract myself, ignore and perhaps even deny. After all, I was lucky enough to have the gift of a new life, any more than that I couldn't expect, (nor had I even considered a *real* possibility, only a dream), and, I told myself, could not have coped with. I was too self-centred, too immature, and after all, only just learning to live and be responsible for myself, let alone take on the responsibility a relationship demands. This seemed very logical, plausible and sensible to me, I thought, until I met Stephen Mann. After our initial introduction, we kept in touch every now and then over the telephone, and then quite suddenly, for both of us, our relationship blossomed into love – and eventually marriage; a great source for self-analysis, thought and debate on my part, as my next chapter shows. Like a horse and carriage go together, so do love and marriage, as they say, but me? ... And Stephen ...?

LOVE AND MARRIAGE

The second time Steve and I actually met (for some time now we had been chatting on the telephone to one another daily), was on 27th February, 1991. I had been admitted into hospital because the bone pain suddenly became intolerable, and, although temporary, I lost all feelings in my legs, and therefore could not move. I'm afraid I remember very little of that evening when he visited – I had had so many drugs injected into me – but I do recall a very kind concerned face, and someone who was willing to listen; someone who from time to time plumped up my pillows, and, when I became uncomfortable, helped to turn me from one side to the other. I also recall his promise to visit the next day, (and also many other relayed-via-nurses telephone messages for a quick recovery from other men friends!) Steve, however, stood out; he had made a hundred mile round trip to visit me – and was coming again.

I have to admit that I didn't think Steve *would* come again. After all it was a long journey, and when it came to tea-time (the time at which he had said he would come), I was certain, although disappointed, that I was right. This, however, turned out to be our first lack of communication. 'Tea-time' to Steve meant evening meal-time – whilst to me it signified the afternoon cuppa, about 3.30ish! So I was somewhat taken aback when in he walked at 5.30 p.m., – armed with flowers, some (beloved) chocolate biscuits, shampoo and tissues. He stayed from 5.30p.m. until midnight! We talked and talked – I was feeling far less drugged – and, with his help and encouragement, (and my

132

embarrassment at having to keep calling for a bed-pan and commode!), I determined to try walking the five metre distance to the loo. I managed it, very unsteadily of course, hanging on to Steve's arm, (any excuse!) – and my stick, causing my knuckles to turn white. When he left, saying he would try and visit again the next day, he helped me into bed and gave me a kiss, which I just couldn't help returning. Goodness knows what went through me at that point – obviously some sort of emotional thrill/excitement, and sexual stirring, but I turned to those chocolate biscuits he had given me after he had gone and ate four in a row! I then tormented myself for some considerable time afterwards! Had that been a 'piggy' thing to do? Or was it being 'normal' or far, far worse – an attempt to stuff back down feelings that were trying to surface? Had I once again reverted to using food as a medium for expression?:

> *'I've just stuffed down 4 chocky biscuits in a row. They were delicious but I do feel a bit icky now. I'm sure I didn't need them. I feel I could eat the whole packet though, too. Oh please, please don't let me choose to restart coping with new emotions in the old familiar way'.*

(Diary 28/2/91)

As it happened, the increase in bone pain and my decrease in pain tolerance coincided with yet another period. The inability to mobilise was, however, just that and coincidental. It unfortunately happens quite a lot today, and is untreatable. The hospital did very many tests to see if I would, or could be, receptive to medication of any kind, but the result was negative, and I am unable to take any strong pain-killers, because, one, of possible constipatory effects and my not wanting to take any more laxatives, and two, because there isn't actually any medication that dulls bone pain, only one's resistance to it, and which makes one very, very drugged indeed. (There again, neither do they prevent any deterioration in the condition). The senior osteopath told me I was welcome to remain in hospital, to enjoy a good rest, for as long as he could spare the bed, but at the same time encouraged me to try and regain my confidence walking, because a little exercise combined with a little rest and high calcium diet, were the only possible 'answers'.

My period having shown signs of starting on 2nd March, I felt very much better emotionally and determined to go back to my flat in a few days. Steve, on hearing of my intention, and having a lot more free time, as it was now a weekend, suggested he take me back to my flat the following day, to help me re-establish myself – catching up on the post and answer-machine messages, as well as unpacking and getting myself an evening meal – to return me to the hospital later, if necessary. It seemed a sensible idea – the build-up of calls having been worrying me – so we had a super afternoon together, on the Sunday, and enjoyed a peanut-butter sandwich and salad picnic and bananas for 'dinner'! I was reluctant to return to the hospital – and Steve having guessed as much whilst also thinking that the forthcoming week might prove a bit formidable, if I stayed in my flat alone, invited me to convalesce for a few days at his home in Hastings. He had two beds; there were no sexual overtones, although we were, by now, holding hands and exchanging the odd kiss, and with a bit of a 'should I shouldn't I' debate going on in my head I agreed. I telephoned the hospital, and my suitcase was suitably repacked!

Stephen, in looking back to that time, has since laughed on many occasions, and me too. There I was flat on my back, clothes off – a position into which many men may spend much time encouraging their partners, – and there he was – trying to get me up on my feet and dressed!

In the event, I stayed with Steve from the 3rd March – 10th March, with a one-day break to Brighton, to check on my flat, spend the evening there, answer yet more build-up of calls, and also to enjoy the following day 'tourist-style' in this seaside town, indulging in breakfast in bed beforehand. Steve had come with me and both of us were feeling that our worlds had been turned upside down. (After that second visit

134

when I ate the four chocolate biscuits, Steve apparently drove home in both moonlight and stardust, and doesn't remember a thing!) On 9th March Steve proposed to me; we were both in a state of shock as a result of that, but equally, so, both sure. We spoke to both his parents, and to Pam and Ron, (now back from the States), and although obviously all were a little dubious, not to mention surprised, were delighted. On 16th March – God, either venting his approval or otherwise, letting the heavens open along with a very dramatic thunder and lightning storm – Steve bought me the most beautiful solitaire diamond engagement ring in the world, with a view to us getting married the following autumn.

It had all been such a whirlwind of a romance that both my diary and logbook took a good bashing, as did self-esteem and self-doubt have a running battle:

> 'My shape means sufficient enough to want to please Steve, and that's about it. Peace of mind, lack of mental anguish, freedom to express emotions is what is most important. Obviously I want to feel proud of my shape, or at least like it, and give Steve some pleasure, but the meaning of my shape is really sliding into insignificance – which is perhaps what it should do. It's not opting out – it's giving me a chance to be, and feel, proud, and look OK.'
>
> (Logbook entry 9/3/91)

> 'I look in the mirror and it's not about shape any more really – it's the whole person that I'm looking at, and generally I feel OK with what and who I see. That's not vanity; it's generally about being happy with who and what I am – free from mental anguish – and, at long last, worthy of both self-respect, and respect from others. Of course, there are a lot of uncertainties about my shape – I cannot see what Steve sees and likes, and I often feel a lack of confidence as he admires/looks at me, but I know it is

135

attractive to him, whilst also knowing that he loves ME *not my shape; my shape is secondary. I'd like a bigger bust now, but I find it easy to laugh – perhaps if I push my tummy in when it sticks out, my boobs will pop out a bit!'*

(Logbook entry 15/3/91)

'Mrs S Mann!! It's the only road I want to go down now, but is this right – putting all my eggs in one basket? I want to give everything to Steve, I cannot hold back, but surely that's not wrong? It's not impulsiveness, it's spontaneity and how can you hold back when you love someone so very much? And this not just sexually. Loving, and receiving love, seems so very, very special – something I never knew existed, let alone be something for me to discover. I hope I can fulfil Steve's every need and desire, but I must, too, keep my own identity. I still find some aspects of making love a little embarrassing; being naked and yet liking Steve to look at me, looking at Steve and touching him and kissing him.'

(Logbook entry 17/3/91)

'Am I really doing the right thing? I know nothing of love. Perhaps it, (mine), is superficial and will wear off? I'm such a self-centred cow, used to living for so long on my own. Perhaps I'm not being fair to Steve? Perhaps I'm just leading him – and myself – up the garden path? Yet another dance?'

(Logbook entry 18/3/91)

Anxieties and doubts abounded, but so did happiness, fun and the wonderful experience of sharing with someone you feel close to. Love increased my feelings of dignity and belongingness. From the official date of our engagement, Steve and I spent all possible time together. Running his own business as an insurance consultant, meant he could not always be certain of being free every evening, so we decided that I would spend Thursdays to Sundays in Hastings, and Steve would travel over on Monday, Tuesday and Wednesday evenings, returning each following morning for work. My telephone help-line was altered according to where I was, my Tuesday self-help group continued to take place, and we were tempted to take out some shares with the Esso company! (My Morris Minor and Steve's Skoda so often hammering down the A27 as we travelled from Brighton to Hastings and Hastings to Brighton!)

At the same time, having by now decided to marry on the first year's anniversary of my leaving anorexia/bulimia nervosa and hospitals behind forever, I put my flat on the market in April. Houses and flats were selling very slowly and we envisaged still having my property in October. However, I sold mine within three days, the exchange of contract to be completed 10th July! So! it was real – or I was going to be homeless! We, and I, in particular, felt we were doing the right thing for both of us, but still my logbook was filled with doubts:

> *'I'm worried about loving Steve enough! I love him so much, but I don't think I can give him enough. It's quite a frightening and powerful emotion, and all-consuming, loving him to this degree. I still find myself becoming embarrassed about my body, but I'm so happy, or is it a novelty? <u>Everything</u> with Steve seems so right/natural/easy. I hope I'll make a good enough wife. I hope, too, I can leave the past behind me, to concentrate on our future. I don't want <u>anything</u> to interfere in our marriage, our life together, but am I strong enough to cope? And will Steve tire of my shortcomings, and emotional weaknesses? I don't want to be a drain or a strain on him. I love him so much. I want to be totally dependent on him in one sense, which it seems I can be, trustways any way, and yet maintain my independence as well, without my wish to control all the time – that way our 'team-work' is bound to fail. Surely it's not what*

I gain, but what I give, that measures the worth of my life?'

(Logbook entry 19/3/91)

Self-torment, self-doubt, self-esteem, self-respect and self-confidence danced around without ceasing, during the period of time leading up to the wedding. Quite normal maybe, as are such self-torments today, but the way I swung from being sure, right into the hands of self-doubt made me feel giddy. Marriage signified to me making a commitment to permanent, unconditional love, which, however, sure I was of our love for one another, felt risky.

Oh! now I know just why I'm here
– in this world, it feels so right.
I do fit in, almost anywhere,
But sometimes I wonder, especially at night.
Can I always be at peace with myself?
I don't always feel good
– sometimes wondering, lonely and misunderstood.
Now somebody loves me,
Someone who cares,
It seems I've found him,
And it's so precious, so rare.
I can't give it all up,
Yet I know I suppose that I could –
Deny myself everything – all that is good.
But I won't, I'll fight,
– but who do I fight?
ME?
Cause me to hurt
And turn away, turn inwards, in fright.
I don't have to pretend to be happy,
'Cos now I'm part of the crowd,
I'm no longer different, or strange,
Nor have need to wear a shroud.
I'll not continue to sit on a shelf
Nor will I envy everyone else.

I've dusted myself down,
Found love, and my smile,
And it's not something that's for 'once in a while'.
This is forever,
Ann! – believe in yourself!
Otherwise you might end up calling 'HELP',
Back on that shelf.
You're free, someone cares,
Stop the doubts and the fears,
Enjoy your life, and keep smiling,
In the warmth of love that's now here.

(Logbook entry 3/4/91)

Having recovered, I realised that neither I nor anybody else has to fit into any category of what people are 'supposed' to be and do. I recognised that we are all unique, and that this individuality is important in marriage, too. Stephen and I would remain our own person with rights and responsibilities.

Another issue that caused me a lot of concern was not so much that of being a 'proper' wife, but of being a good enough daughter-in-law, and, therefore, being accepted by Steve's parents. (Steve being an only child too). When I first met Mum and Dad, (Gladys and Frank Mann), I experienced no apparent problems, but as they, like Steve, began to love me I became terrified. I felt I'd failed as a daughter, and that as a daughter-in-law, I would fail again. I love my parents-in-law very much indeed, if only because when I tried to explain to them how I was feeling, they showed an extraordinary amount of tolerance, but their love remained intimidating. Being accepted was intimidating, too, because, most of all, I thought they would then have expectations of me, and having always tried to be a 'people-pleaser', I could see myself doing things for the family first, and myself afterwards – and failing. It was a very definite feeling of insecurity, because, when finding the road to recovery, I had thought that the emotional links between food and caring could, and possibly had, become confused with insecurity

around parenting and my fears around eating. I was determined, although scared stiff, to try and conquer this fear, but
at times I was too weak. Steve and I experienced several
tearful goodbyes, because the one thing I would not, and
could not do, was alienate him from his, (very loving) family,
and occasionally I just felt I could not go visit them. (They
live locally to us; about three miles away). I never actually
walked out of the door on these occasions, but certainly my
case was packed and unpacked many times.

I suppose, in these instances of self-doubt, I was forgetting
our relationship was a *team* effort, which meant working and
sharing *together*. I was also forgetting that love takes time in
its demanding a history of giving and receiving, laughing and
crying, and supposing a willingness to struggle, to work, to
suffer and join in rejoicing together. In respect of shying
away from Stephen's family, I was taking the whole thing on
myself. I had forgotten about asking for help, and had
temporarily forgotten that it was not just me now, but *us*.
Until I was able to 'come clean' entirely over this issue, my
logbook and diary once again took a good thrashing:

> *'I feel very uncomfortable in the company of Steve's
> parents, with whom I'm obviously at the same time
> going to become closely involved … I am anxious
> that, for them, I won't be a very successful Mrs
> Mann.'*
>
> (Logbook entry 13/4/91)

> *'I experience so much anxiety re being accepted,
> (and being successful), as a daughter by Steve's
> parents. Having a 'Mum and Dad', and being a
> nice/liked daughter. I've never succeeded before, and
> no doubt there will be expectations. After all, surely,
> expectations are normal?'*
>
> (Logbook entry 20/4/91)

> *'I'm sure I'll never be a good enough friend, lover
> and wife to Steve, nor daughter-in-law to 'Mum and*

140

Dad'. I'm worried about the relationship between myself and Steve's parents, and therefore the way this might affect the relationship between Steve and his parents. Can I really become part of a family – be successful and loved – and not fail?'

(Logbook entry 10/5/91)

'Becoming part of Steve's family seems to be a problem. Being loved I find intimidating and frightening. I failed as a daughter, – I don't want failure again. The torment keeps coming – leave Steve, break off our relationship, – otherwise I might drive the family apart; be a wedge between Steve and his parents, by either (i) keeping my distance, and (ii) keeping Steve at a distance from his parents, too. The guilt would just rear its' head. What would I do when Steve visited his parents? Where would I go? What excuses could he (continue to) make? I couldn't just stay in Steve's house, – not going would be a failure. It's a catch 22! Yet I'm not sure I have enough courage to tell Steve's parents because they are bound to deny they have any expectations, which is understandable, but it's human nature to have them. Surely?'

(Logbook entry 15/5/91)

Despite all this turmoil, though, I was able to make the following entry in my diary a few days later, to Steve:

'I realise that the most beautiful thing is not a sunset, but the joy of sharing it together. Going to the park, smelling hyacinths, seeing bluebells, poppies and pansies, as well as walking, laughing, talking and listening. Just holding hands. Asking about each others' day. Being proud of each others' accomplishments. A feeling of being incomplete when we are apart.

Giving a part of myself, makes me feel whole.

141

Sharing a laugh, a sadness, a moment. This is what life is about now. A relationship which encompasses friendship, but that is something special which we know we've got. People call it 'love', I guess, but I think that word is too loosely used. Only we know the depths of this emotion, and perhaps only me, its' power, because sometimes I feel I need to DESTROY *and not share; I feel inadequate, hurt and vulnerable'.*

And, on 31st May 1991, wrote in my logbook:

'To be constructive, I think family relationships, from now on, have to focus on Steve and his family, and me. No-one else. Not what wasn't or what was, – except, of course, where appropriate, Pam and Ron. I have no-one else. I still feel intimidated by Steve's parents' love for me, – not by them as individuals. It is nothing personal. It is a failure on my part; I expect I would be the same with anyone. I have no idea who I am, nor what I am, at times, nor what is my rôle in this respect. I dread their expectations. I must go on, as myself, to the best of my ability and remember that, so far, anyway, I am liked and loved for who I am and what I am, not for what I do'.

In order to avoid parting, Steve and I tried 'to solve' my fears by sharing them with my in-laws, thus making the 'team' a larger one and a family one, and indeed this did, and does, help. I felt no pressures, but there is still a little hesitancy on my part, even today – to visit them on my own. They love me so much! It seems so crazy to be frightened by the one thing I have always wanted, but in the beginning as I started my journey of discovery, it was such an unknown quantity, and beyond even Steve's comprehension. (And it is still a bit of a stranger at times today.) Their love seems to instantly hit me when I'm in their company, and it just knocks me for six. Perhaps it is the issue of control again, because I have not as yet accepted any of their invitations to have a meal with them. I cannot pinpoint the exact reason for this, because we have wined and dined together quite frequently, both in our home and out, but obviously sharing things together, a meal, conversation, and company in this instance, in an intimate way, on their 'territory', holds some intimidating connotations, which must centre around this issue of love, surely, because no-one else's 'territory' frightens me.

The most wonderful thing about the relationship between Stephen and myself is that, first and foremost, Steve is my best friend, and me, his. We met as friends, have remained as such, and since becoming man and wife, love has grown and continued to grow and blossom daily. Sometimes I feel Steve cannot possibly love me any more, and therefore can only love me less, but he doesn't. He may not like me all the time, (I do nag a bit sometimes!), but he continues to love me more, and I, for my part, as in one of Dr Hook's records, and to my amazement, too, often turn to him and say, 'When you think I've loved you all that I can, then I'll love you a little bit more.' I, too, feel I cannot possibly love Steve any more, but the fantastic thing is that this emotion is ongoing, and grows, just like Topsy. So I do!

Having met Steve and seen our relationship develop, so my diary and logbook ceased to be used so much. As Steve replaced my diary and logbook's role of best friend, so it was with him that I shared and share most things, although not everything – presents and secrets for example I still continued to share with my diary alone! I more or less stopped my writings in September of 1991, mainly in the first instance because the wedding preparations were demanding a lot of time and work, and travelling back and forth (from Hastings then, since as of 10th July, I had been living with Steve), to Bournemouth, where we had chosen to be married. I do not honestly know wether that was right or wrong. Certainly I have become less serious about myself and less self-analytical, which is not a bad thing as I'm always alert to any possibility of using the old coping mechanisms, but I do experience build-ups, (sometimes unconsciously so), of anxieties, tensions and fears, and it is only in retrospect that I realise that had I turned to my logbook and diary, I might have prevented such a high degree of emotional distress. On the other hand, if I wrote as I did, I feel there would be a danger of not communicating fully with Steve. But of course, this is putting myself in my old familiar 'no win' situation! What I try to do is adopt a middle line, and write occasionally when I feel a muddle in my head, and talk to Steve about it afterwards. I, also, from time to time, read past entries, and can see familiar thoughts and behavioural patterns, which is an invaluable asset for further understanding. So, whatever, my logbook and diary will remain my very close personal friends.

Although the issue of my shape and its meaning became less and less important, and is almost insignificant today, the first few months with Steve saw it actually become a little *more* problematic than it had been since the previous year. I could not understand why he liked to look at my body, liked what he could see and wanted to touch and caress it all over; nor, in fact, *what* he could see, and my lack of understanding encompassed some fear and embarrassment, at times channelled through feelings of being fat. This was another hurdle I determined to come to grips with, or rather one where I knew we *both* had to work together in order to achieve that goal. We therefore decided to bath together and have 'mirror sessions', as I did when I was in the clinic. In that way, I, too, could look at what Steve saw and liked, and try and understand why – and perhaps, feel a little more self-esteem. It was a very wise decision this, particularly the mirror work, because I learned a lot about my and other female bodies. I began to appreciate curves and shapes as a part of me; that they didn't just look OK and lovely on other ladies, but were also a part of *my* body. And at this point love-making began to take on a much deeper, greater feeling of giving and receiving love and pleasure. However, the course was never completely smooth from the onset of that decision. There were still days when I channelled my emotions the old way:

> *'Shape has recently been a problem. Having a bath was difficult – I had to ask Steve to turn off the light! I felt so awful. Not fat but ugly, and today I feel pretty horrible too, – so thick-waisted and lumpy. My breasts are quite full and rounded, (for me!), but I don't mind that now, – it quite pleases me to have a 'ledge'* (our family word for my chest, because after eating there are always a few crumbs on it!) *It's my tummy that has been concerning me, and likewise, with the warmer weather and wearing short-sleeved and sleeveless T-shirts, my thick wrists and arms. However, on the whole, I think I have 'shape', although important, in more or less the right perspective. Thoughts are being (angrily) channelled through this medium at the moment because of three reasons:-*
> 1. *My move, and therefore adapting to a new life.*
> 2. *Pam and Ron having now emigrated, to join their daughter and her family in the States, although I suppose I should see that as a positive move, because they obviously think I'm well, and believe in me.*
> 3. *The wedding – and yet another new life-style.'*
> (Logbook entry 31/7/91)

As a rule I was always, and fairly quickly, able to trace the trigger of my thoughts to an emotion, and tracing the trigger remains the key today. Fortunately, I'm quite a dab hand now! – but equally so the old anorectic thought patterns are fading, albeit a very long and die-hard process, and also I have many other constructive outlets for my emotions, – crying, laughing, swearing(!), and telling someone just how I *do* feel about something they have done, truthfully, to name but a few. I also enjoy bashing a pillow or cushion, and poking Umber (our cat) with my walking stick – who, incidentally, thinks its a game and enjoys it as such!

145

Two particular die-hard patterns of thought, though, were (and are sometimes today), deserving and enjoying; hence there was a lot of pushing and pulling in our relationship. I found dealing with all these good, exciting events, from my recovery process all the way to meeting and becoming engaged to Steve, too much to handle. It was like indulging in too much ice cream again, and the only way I could think of coping with it all was to deny myself some, by throwing it away. Again, of course, I was trying to solve things rather than enjoy experiencing, so I immediately started denying myself Steve's love. This took all manner of (alarming) forms, and caused Steve much pain, but when I saw the tears rolling down his face, I would not let myself feel any compassion. In fact, I didn't care, or at least told myself I didn't. Every time it happened, and as the build-up to the wedding increased, so it occurred with even more intensity, even including a few bouts of 'fisty cuffs' as Steve tried to prevent me going out the front door, case packed! For both of us there were a lot of issues centred around this pushing and pulling which we had to discuss, and yet although seeking some advice from the Reverend Paul Renyard, who blessed our marriage, we still felt sure in our heart of hearts about marrying. On my part, I had to consider whether or not there was more to this than denying myself something, because I was also upsetting, and hurting, someone else. Did I want to 'wear the trousers' perhaps, even though we both described our relationship as a team? Or even worse still, I felt there was something vicious in me that yearned to hurt a man. My father had hurt me – was I therefore, trying to hurt him back through Steve? And/or trying to assure myself that no man could or would control me or my life? I had my own identity and was my own person and determined to remain so. Steve was, and is, in no way a threatening person, nor is he demanding – unlike my father for example – so it didn't entirely make sense that I should so viciously attack him. Obviously I was hurting myself too, but if I wanted to hurt just me, surely I could have chosen some other avenue? Knowing I loved Steve, it seemed so odd to exhibit such antagonistic behaviour, and, even though aware of what I was doing, seemingly be unable to control it. Love, I had always appreciated, was costly, which was why I suppose I had avoided it for twenty-eight years, however, this cost was proving very dear.

Steve for his part, had to do some very serious soul-searching, too. Was he hanging on to me because of the challenge it presented? Did he really love me? After all it would be so much easier to be free of all this pain and hassle. Were his feelings for me more sympathy than love? Knowing my physical limitations and living alone could he just let me go back to Brighton to try and cope? (And this would, by now, encompass looking for a new residence). Or, and this was, I understand, his greatest inner battle, was he being selfish? He had been on his own for long enough to know he disliked it. He wanted to share his life with someone, and although firmly believing that someone must be out there, but a someone he began to think he was obviously not going to meet, he had become something of a workaholic and lonely. Until now. These issues he solved relatively easily, so I'm told. If he didn't love me, he explained, then none of these questions would have arisen. It would have been simple. There would have been no physical struggles, or tugs-of-war. He would just have opened the door and waved me off, and would have been glad to see the back of me. Having thus reached his own peace of mind, he determined to go on fighting to keep our relationship, but made it quite clear he would and could not keep me a prisoner, forever locked in. I was free to leave, he was not my jailer and I was free to come back, or stay away, as I wished, but, whatever, he would always love me and miss me.

In some ways, although Steve was not consciously playing devil's advocate, this shed a different light on things – being able to leave. I didn't have to stay! But still determined to deny myself all this wonderful life and choice now – go or stay – I left twice. The first occasion was when Steve received an emergency call to go to Accident and Emergency because his mother had cut herself very badly, and the second, when

147

I went 'out shopping'. I had always said that if I left I would never take the keys with me, I would never return, I had committed myself and I was not going to cry wolf by continuing to leave and return when it suited me or when I felt the need. Both of these occasions were without Steve's knowledge, and although pre-planned were also opportunist 'escapes'. However, they both failed. Perhaps it was fate, who knows? On the first occasion my car broke down midway between Hastings and Brighton, and Steve, pursuing me, when he returned from the hospital, in his own car, found me stranded on the dual carriage way awaiting the AA! And the second time, I fell heavily in the street, knocking my head as I went down, thus ending up in A and E myself, where, of course, identification, address, etc was all discovered!

In a way, although very emotionally painful and bizzare, it was also rather funny. Just as I couldn't die when I was ill, so now, I couldn't leave Steve. It was a paradox but with a slight difference, because as the pushing and pulling continued – including me, on two occasions, taking a rather hearty dose of sleeping medication to try and sleep away the confusion – we became closer than ever. Our love grew, our relationship strengthened and we learned a lot, about one another, and love and living. In our decision to marry, and hence our determination to hang on in there, we experienced more highs and lows than ever before, in all our lifetimes put together. Both of us wanted security, and both being very tactile, holding hands, hugs and kisses mean a lot to us. I would often deny Steve these things, yet at the same time long for him to grab my hand, or insist upon hugging me. I had been fighting to have the power, yet longed to relinquish it. I wanted control, yet I also wanted all the responsibilities to be taken away from me, and be wrapped up in cotton wool. It was a kind of back-to-front language of saying 'no' when I meant 'yes'. Perhaps I felt my independence and own identity were going to be taken away from me again, and that I might be smothered? I still didn't understand fully this thing called 'unconditional love', and meanwhile let slip

148

quite a bit of my self-confidence and self-respect, and, yes, channelled it through body-shape and size for a while in a complete sea of self-doubt and bewilderment.

The most vehement pushing and pulling sessions, it seemed for a while, over a short spate of time, showed a small pattern. One pattern linked into my periods – mid-cycle time and a few days before the period showed, when my hormones as the doctor put it 'somersaulted in turmoil'. (As I had not experienced menstruation since my teens, and then only for a short while, my body and moods, even though belonging to a thirty nine year old, apparently were typical of puberty). The second pattern, we noticed, appeared to follow a good time, whether that be several days without any pushing or pulling on my part, or a lovely day, or evening out, or something far more simple yet enjoyable. Like a whiplash 'it' than hit out or back, almost as if enjoyment involved cost. It reeked of parallels in the past, like not being able to celebrate promotion, and it could have become a psychological scare, showing something of that anorectic attitude. However, we determined it would not. It was no use not planning to have fun in case of a whiplash; we had to learn to cope. And I had to learn that there need be no cost, only my own charge. Good feelings were free.

It would have been easy to put a lot of my behaviour down to extenuating circumstances – for example, the wedding. And many people, Stephen included, my in-laws, the Reverend Renyard, a good friend and Pam and Ron did just that. I, on the other hand, felt it to be something far more than the typical pre-wedding 'scratchy and tearful' period. I didn't trust myself and, I suppose, I didn't and couldn't believe I was normal. The pitfalls of self-doubt seemed like great caverns at times, and I felt so inadequate, yet as each bout and pitfall occurred, so Steve and I saw it as a constructive learning experience, and paradoxically we became closer than ever, and our love more intense. Not because we felt we were hanging on to each other in desperation – which we did indeed consider – but because we always came through together as a team and felt more positive. I, too, gradually, with the help of my logbook and diaries began to realise what I was doing – although anorexia nervosa was history, the old thought patterns and behaviour were still occasionally around. My emotional scars had not, and I daresay have not, completely disappeared, and at times they surfaced and I re-experienced what we began to call 'inside pain', ('outside pain' referred to my physical disability). Try as I might, I could not explain my inside hurt to Steve – or for that matter write it in my logbook and diary in order that he might read it and perhaps understand. My words seemed inadequate – Stephen could not *feel* my hurt, be empathic to it or identify with it, and so possibly, in my frustration, I tried to project my feelings onto him by hurting him. (Naturally he wouldn't experience all my hurt.) It was a very vicious, emotional, game-like attack that I was playing and I knew it, so I told him and this did in fact help Steve a lot. For one he could see that it was the die-hard coping mechanisms raising their heads, which after such a long illness and way of life, was only to be expected, and two, he was able to be more objective and become less emotional. 'However hard you try to hurt me or make me hate you', he said, 'you will never succeed. I love you too much. Sticks and stones may break my bones but your words will never hurt me. I have never felt such love from someone, as I do you, nor have I ever loved someone as I do you. I believe in myself, I believe in you, and I believe in us', he told me one day.

Thankfully, the pushing and pulling is now well faded, but not until quite recently, and certainly not immediately after the build-up to, and the actual wedding itself. For some time I could feel the strong urges of wanting to go, wanting to run away to be free, wanting to be alone, which was not a simple need of wanting my own space. (After all I had a ready-packed suitcase). Perhaps it was the paradox of the strong love binding us. When the world seemed a bit of a difficult place in which to be, and our love seemed bigger than both of us, I felt the need to deprive myself. It was a coping mechanism I had used so well in the past. Yet Steve and I never felt smothered by one another; we maintained our own interests and our own individuality, and respected and respect one another should either of us feel the need to be on our own.

The main point was that in being aware of the dangers of living for one another solely, living in one another's shoes, and as one psychologist I know would have described it 'living in one another's knickers' so we became aware that when the strong urges to go, to leave came, I had to ride with, and experience those feelings, not try to solve them. They were a part of my recovery process, which, like it or not, was to be ongoing for a very long time. Self-denial did not work – I had learned that from my eating disorder, and 'normal' life was still quite new. On top of that, I had sold my own home, moved into a new one, and had married, as well as continued with the help-line, made various radio broadcasts and TV appearances and started two self-help groups! There was a huge amount of ice cream on my plate and I had to acknowledge it, by enjoying and savouring it a little at a time, at my own pace, in order to learn what being a woman and a wife was all about. There were no duties, as such, but I was learning to share – physically, emotionally and spiritually. I was learning to live with someone and take into account their needs as well as mine, (which inevitably involved compromise), and I was learning to try keep house for two. I was learning to *ADAPT* and become more flexible, (rigidity being foremost in my eating disorder), along with learning about, and trying to cope with, the more personal aspects of womanhood. Talk about in at the deep end! And this was something about which I constantly had to remind myself when self-doubt loomed, and something which Steve, too, saw as a right about which to remind me, almost in reprimand form. When he felt I was setting too high a goal, in order, perhaps, to be a perfect wife, or was looking to do things well all the time, he would comment and remind me that I deserved to rest too – I didn't have to prove my worth by proving my usefulness.

The issues of being a 'good wife' and 'feeling useful' were something else that took a long time with which to come to terms. First of all, of course, there is no definition of a 'good wife', and 'feeling useful' doesn't warrant doing or proving all the time. An early entry in my logbook (4th April 1991) showed the fears that were continuing, but also my awareness:

> *'Self-doubt and self-esteem still vie for top position! but then I guess that's normal. However, self-doubt can certainly be destructive. My confidence goes, and self-value and self-worth to a lesser extent, which is more obvious when I'm away from the helpline and not 'working'. 'Working' has its therapeutic side in that I feel useful and I get such positive, rewarding feedback. Doing/being nothing is too dangerous – it allows room for self-doubt, but then I'm not a nobody even if I'm not working. I'm ME and I like me, and I feel OK about myself. When I look in the mirror these days it's not a matter of vanity; quite simply I'm content with what I see – the mental anguish has gone. I feel socially acceptable and love being a woman. I love being feminine – at long last. I don't want to lose it, but still I find it excruciatingly embarrassing when Steve looks at me and touches me, and says how lovely I am. Yet I like to hear this, despite not being able to see it. Perhaps I'm just seeking approval and reassurance all the time? I love how he loves me, and I hope one day I'll be able to prove to him the 100% I love him. Sometimes I guess I must seem rather inadequate, stupid and clumsy, I don't know how to prove things. Few people trusted me when I was ill, including myself, so how do I prove things now?'*

I feel that being so physically disabled was certainly a contributory factor in all this, but not the single factor – I've always been a 'doer' and have always sought reassurance, this perhaps being my much needed proof. Adapting to being fully retired was much more traumatic than I had ever considered. In fact, I had never seriously considered the full implications. I remember during my working years that a system of 'training for retirement' had been introduced to colleagues to cover their last couple of years. This, apparently, was to help them gradually 'wind down' and adapt to, if not a less active life, then certainly a different daily lifestyle, without any imposed structure and pressure; structure and routine often playing an important part in daily living. It certainly was mine! Now, however, not only were my days different, but I also had to cope with the physical limitations of being registered physically disabled. Having a bath, washing my hair, general household work, such as changing and making beds, doing the washing and ironing and dusting and hoovering, are sometimes completely impossible, and I need help. Hence, possibly, my feelings of inadequacy about being a good wife'. What if I couldn't keep up with the washing and ironing? – I couldn't let Steve go to work in dirty or creased un-ironed clothes, and what about the house? Polishing, dusting, spring-cleaning and hoovering had to be done. I couldn't expect my husband to come home to all this after a days' work. And what about cooking – not dropping things, not burning things and providing a meal encompassing both a varied and nutritional diet?

These niggles obviously chased around in my head, and when I fell, or was tired, they often got completely out of proportion. Eventually I shared my worries, and Steve adopted the Pollyanna hat so we could look at the good in the bad, and laugh. Crumpled clothes – they were the 'in' thing weren't they? – the 'creased look'. As for the washing, we reckoned we could easily survive a month without difficulty, and anyway Steve was quite capable of filling and emptying a washing machine in five minutes. It wasn't necessarily my job. As for cooking that was no big deal either. We already had three weeks worth of pre-prepared meals in the freezer, which I had, over a period of time, built up in various 'baking sessions', and, apart from that, if we were not eating a meal from there, Steve loved surprises. (One of his favourite being cheesy mashed potato with baked beans there was always a rescue menu in the larder, not to mention the fish and chip shop and chinese take-away a few yards away from us next-door but two!) Further, Steve considered none of these jobs to be solely mine; they may be associated with a housewife, but they did not constitute the meaning of a wife. As far as he was concerned I was the best wife in the world, because I was his friend, his confidante, his strength and someone who gave and received a lot of love. I was flummoxed! I couldn't see how, and for a small period showered Steve with little gifts to justify all that he said about me loving him and giving to him. I could see what I was doing – trying to present something tangible so that I could measure my feelings for him and prove them. As well as this, of course, I felt it might make up for my physical inadequacies. Perhaps I also thought it might make me feel a little better about myself. It did none of this, needless to say, although I naturally experienced much pleasure in buying things for Steve, but it did work in a very paradoxical fashion. (Paradoxes were becoming the 'story of my life'!) Steve felt very privileged to be given these presents from time to time, but also guilty in that, as he saw it, I was always so thoughtful, whilst beyond regular bunches of flowers, he never thought to buy me any surprises. I told him it didn't matter, I didn't need or want them, he gave me so much already – himself. Suddenly I then understood what he had been saying, – that it was ME he loved, and he loved me for being me, not for my clean, well-ironed shirts and hankies, a shining house and cordon bleu meals. I finally grasped this thing called love, and from then on found it far easier to accept my limitations, and gracefully so. And my confidence and belief in myself became stronger than ever. For so many years, whilst ill, I had blamed people for only hearing and not listening, quite a common human trait, and I realised that concerning these issues, this was just what I had been doing. The realisation hurt, but it was a lesson well learned, because I also stopped, in my worst moments of doubt, trying to persuade both myself and Steve that somewhere there must be someone for him who would be 'better' than

me. I realised, and kept remembering, that our love is unconditional, so that sort of thinking is not really to the point.
What is, is that he chose me, and I chose him – for being
ourselves.

Until I lived with Steve, I had been rigidly following my
three-weekly menu cycle: one, because as I said before, it was
a safeguard, and two, it suited my purse. However, with all
the different sorts of foods around these days, I was not
being very adventurous and I was still very much a novice
cook. As our relationship grew, so I became more confident
about trying out new dishes, if only because Steve has different preferences to me, (although we share many favourites),
and several dislikes! At first, I was very nervous, not at all
because of the calorie content, (I stopped counting calories
the moment I entered the clinic), nor the nutritional content,
but whether I was eating enough. What, I puzzled, constituted a serving or portion? It was easy to judge the amount
when it came to 'straightforward' fish, chips and peas, or
shepherds pie with potato and vegetables, for example, but a
plate of lasagne was a very different matter, so in telling
Steve we hung on together, trying to differentiate between
my feelings of irrational fear and being full-up, and fear of
being left hungry!

Of course, I also relied upon my regular weighing sessions,
which I continued when I moved to Hastings, so between
everything, with a few misses, I, or rather we, I suppose, got
the right balance. Gradually this became less and less of a
problem and priority – although I still experience difficulty
today in recognising hunger and thirst – and I have become
a very adventurous, flexible and, apparently, 'superb' cook,
who actually enjoys it as a hobby, because in baking and
conjuring up some home-ideas, I create something.

Mind you, I'm very reluctant to tell Steve what we are
having for dinner if he asks, because my experiments are still
sometimes a bit hit and miss, leaving a lot of guesswork.
Particularly with regard timing and quantities! On Shrove
Tuesday for example, the savoury stuffed pancakes were
delicious, but the sweet unstuffed ones, which I had reheated

for the same amount of time as the former, were, well! – I described them as burnt, they were BLACK, – but Steve bravely munched on, describing them as 'just a bit crunchy'! We have also, or rather Steve has (I had to give up!), chewed our way through undercooked and thus semi-raw shepherds pie – with a touch too much garlic, (well a clove or two too much, actually), and a very rubbery omelette! Of course me being me, I tended to see these occasions as failures, so I had to look hard for Pollyanna. She wasn't far away – just around the corner usually – and I soon began to see the amusing side. Cooking disasters are quite commonplace, generally speaking, so I understand, (my dear mum-in-law has listed many!) but I wanted to make something of mine. It could be thrown away, (there was the chippy and the chinky just along the road, and baked beans in the cupboard) or it could all be put into a saucepan, to heat through/cook a little more/thicken or thin down. By adding various ingredients such as sauces, cheese and vegetables it could become a 'mystery slosh' and a satisfactory rescue mission, which we could do together and thoroughly enjoy! Strangely enough, since then, since taking the rescue attitude we have had very few 'sloshes', but we do have a lot of 'Ah'. You see, I'm still seeking more confidence and success in my cooking, and am always doubtful that my experiments will work, although I'm very eager and willing to give it a go, so when Steve enquires as to what the evening meal is, my response is usually 'Ah'! Although he jokes at being sick and tired of 'Ah', it's wonderful to hear him telling other people he has never eaten so well in his life, nor has he had such variety. And as for me, 'Ah' has done a lot – I have become far more flexible and relaxed. I feel comfortable with experimenting with unknown entities, and although I plan our meals in advance, (more to coincide with my shopping sprees as well as maximise the house-keeping to its best), I can adapt quite easily. Should anyone suddenly drop in, or come to stay, I can actually say that without any difficulty at all, I can always whip up something, and quickly. (And not baked beans!).

It would be totally untrue to say that this flexibility developed overnight. It was gradual and there were initially great difficulties in using a frying-pan, because of the childhood memories it evoked, and the fat. I determined to conquer this, but Steve and I had to do it together, and many attempt ended in tears, and me fleeing the kitchen, terrified. Finally, however, with patience, determination and Stephen's encouragement I've completely overcome this and we enjoy omelettes, and ham, egg and chips quite regularly, although I've yet to master getting the omelette just as we like it – not too set, and not too runny – each time!

19th October, 1991, our wedding day, came and went very quickly, but it was for both of us of course one of our most memorable days. I wore a fairy godmother length, ivory coloured, 1950s style, wedding dress, showing off my legs without the tubi-grip, (which I had been wearing for almost a year in order to mobilise), and matching satin shoes with a little heel. This was a great achievement because I had been determined from the onset to walk down the aisle in a pair of high-heeled shoes, and not wearing a full-length gown. (We had agreed, however, that should a wheelchair be necessary it would be decorated all over, and no doubt, to do it in real style, we would swap it for a bright red wheelbarrow!)

To accompany me were Sue, Jo and Gail, my three beautiful bridesmaids; the sun shone, although the wind blew, (creating many difficulties with my veil, and the bridesmaids' dress collars), and the church was full. We were overwhelmed by the number of people attending the church blessing, (both of us having been married before could not, under Church of England ruling, be married in church so we had had a register office ceremony earlier that morning), and by the kindness of St Barnabas' congregation who gave us our reception, (providing quiches, salads, desserts, gateaux, trifles as well as the two-tiered, most beautiful and superb tasting wedding cake). They have always shown us both so much love and consideration.

The service was very moving – many people remarked on this, and have since said that they have never experienced

157

anything quite like it, regarding both the service and the reception. Of course, being a service of blessing, not marriage, made it different from the start for most people, but love abounded everywhere, and LOVE was the theme we chose for the service. Everywhere shone with it, as well as the love that apparently exuded, and still does exude from us. This has been described as a very wonderful gift that we give to others. What a compliment! Neither of us is quite sure what we do; for both of us being married and being able to give and receive was our own personal bonus, (the receiving part for me, more so, because at long last my barriers had gone, and I was at last free to receive), but to learn that *our* personal bonus gives something to *other* people was absolutely astonishing, although of course, very wonderful too. A double bonus then, which has become self-perpetuating, and which is always ongoing.

Now settled into our new life, I can still only describe life as fun, despite the normal ups and downs. As well as frequently taking photographs, we have a 'Fun Book' in which we enter fun moments. These are not just special occasions, for example birthdays, or visits to the theatre, but other occasions when perhaps we have had to look for Pollyanna, and look upon something as a constructive learning experience, which, although painful at the time, ended in fun. For example an entry on 16th April 1992 reads:

> '*A bad spell for last few days, but we treated it as a learning experience through which we have to come together, in order to be stronger and closer. We celebrated with tea at Tescos – passion cake and coffee – a bottle of wine, a soppy video, a bubble bath, an easy cook-together-dinner, and made love in the most tenderest of ways'.*

This, compared with a diary entry on 16th April *1991*:

> '*Tried to get Steve to feel I'm a bloody nuisance. I'm so tired and just don't give or do enough.*

Perhaps he'll realise I'm not quite the 'fun loving lady' he has always described me as and agree to end our relationship. The hurt would be less now, than if we part after marrying. He adamantly refused though! He says he loves me and then I push harder. Where is the good in this? – I'm finding it so difficult to spot.'

Compared, too, to, if nothing else to show the recovery process had moved forwards, a logbook entry on 16th April 1990:

'I'd like to live now, but I know that I can't,
I'd like to be normal, but I know that I shan't.
I'd like to be slim, but I'll always be fat,
And I ain't got 9 lives, I'm not a cat.
I'm a person who is trying desperately to laugh,
But who knows that really, inside, it's a farce.
I cannot find fun, I only shed tears
I'm a misery, and gloomy, I've had enough of
    life's years.'

In concluding this particular chapter, I can only say that (our) marriage is a wonderful institution. Having now experienced love, I feel I can rightfully say that my life is meaningful. John Powell, Professor of Loyola University, Chicago, believes love is a life-wager. Me, too. Loving, and being loved is the key, and I think it is for everyone, although – as I constantly have to remind myself – the promise is not always instant gratification. Rather ultimate fulfilment. The fun of finding fun(!) in just everyday norm, is not difficult, and the fun of creating a home together, and sharing our life, even with its worries, our concerns and 'down' periods, is always very special. We don't always like one another, of course, (especially, as far as I am concerned, Steve, when he continually forgets to squeeze out the dishcloth, and, consequently I go to use a cold yucky cloth, which drips down my arm and all over the floor!), but we do always *love* one

159

another. Dissension of any kind, especially family dissension, upsetting me as a child and during those years of illness, I have actively had to remember that when things between us go awry, it is not a threat to our marriage, even though my boat may feel very rocked. I have had to learn to accept that there may be days when disagreements and disturbing emotions might come between us. As well as psychological and physical miles separate us. We will not always be able to read one another correctly, either, and so misjudge one another's needs, and we do not always remember everything. Trying to get it right, or be perfect, all the time is wrong, and not necessary. I know now that I can, and will, fail – be it due to lack of wisdom or an abundance of self-weakness – but this is allowed (for Steve, too) because in our commitment to each other we know full well our intention. To always love one another; I will always love Stephen, and he me.

Life, for me is all about putting our relationship first, without feeling guilty, because it is necessary that we have time and space for one another to grow together, and remain strong in our relationship. Of course, trying to help other people, concerning the world of eating disorders, is important too, so I have continued with my help-line, self-help group, counselling and interview, and I am also wise to the fact that in order to retain our own identities and avoid the ruts, we must continue to follow our own interests. Mine include writing, sewing, visiting my friends for little daytime 'soirees' and following sport, particularly the Winter Olympics and tennis, whilst Steve's include DIY, reading, his tropical fish and browsing round garden centres. (Together we share a love of gardening, walking, visiting the local theatre, music, shopping and oh! many, many other more simple pleasures, such as just talking to one another.)

There is another important thing of which I'm always aware, too. I feel privileged to be here, even during the down times, – I'm alive, and I'm privileged to be alive and be experiencing living and loving, to the full, which, in my marriage is summed up by the chorus from a well known song:

'You got to cry a little, laugh a little.
That's the glory of, that's the story of love.'

And that's us! – we do cry and laugh together – a lot.

TODAY AND YESTERDAY: LOOKING BACK

Since recovering and becoming well, my appreciation of all life's diversities and extremes has mellowed. I have become far more aware of life's fragilities, and considerably more tolerant of its and other peoples' imperfections. Each second, just alive and breathing, and free from the mental anguish has taken on an added value, compared with so many years feeling crippled with despair, longing for the whole thing to end – and just wondering and waiting. It makes me truly consider that tragedy does indeed shape character. These days, whenever I awake – even if it is because of the physical pain – it signifies the greatness of another day dawning, and I thank God for it. If I hadn't suffered anorexia nervosa, would I, I often wonder, have ever reached this pinnacle?

Now, well, each day seems sweeter than ever. Waking each morning is fantastic; walking round the park, tending to our garden, smelling the flowers, finding and seeing new friends – all this has acquired a new depth. The content of each day is so rich now, but the pains in my legs, hips and spine sometimes drag me down. Especially as this has been combined with all sorts of hormonal changes and demands as my body chugs back into normality. After twenty two years without a period, my poor old system goes into shock and completely haywire, as every month I acknowledge my feminity! I'm very proud to be a normal woman, but sometimes pain overtakes. However, Stephen is always there to try and help me to draw back. At times, since sharing with him absolutely everything, in which nobody else does, or can ever share, he and I have had to cling on for all we are

162

worth. Loving someone and feeling their love for me is a totally new, and sometimes, still frightening experience. When I hurt inside, it is my reaction, more often than not, to forget that I *can* now share, so instead, like a wounded animal, I retreat, and go into a corner, into myself, to lick my own wounds. The depth of our love has brought out so much emotion in me that at times it has been too over-whelming – to the degree that I feel giddy and faint! I cannot always take all the wonderment, joy and love on board, and, like the wounded animal in the corner, do not want a hug or cuddle. Looking back at the times when I've wondered if Steve and I should part, during those pushing and pulling moments, I can see it's me just walking or running away again – to nothing. And running/walking away has been what anorexia was about. I could never put down roots, and I could never stay with my feelings.

I feel the core of any eating disorder is self-deprivation and a feeling of hatred and desperation. It was mine. The ritualistic and obsessional behavioural patterns, with food and otherwise, were my emotional release from situations that were difficult to handle.

In numbing myself through sheer starvation, or creating the euphoria and 'buzz' that goes with excessive exercising, bingeing, vomiting and purging, the world became OK. But only temporarily and it became shorter and shorter lived. Everything became submerged in confusion; I wanted one thing, was taking another, thinking one thing and saying something else.

I do now know some, if not all of the underlying issues of my illness, but it is impossible to share everything with everybody. It would hurt me too much, and it might hurt others more, because of misinterpretation than anything else. Blame is so often apportioned and is the one thing that should be avoided. It is neither appropriate or necessary. Although an eating disorder is a lonely isolated one, it is, on the whole, family orientated, unfortunately manifesting itself in one member, and the family should recognise their part in it, even if the cold realisation is that they are dysfunctional

163

as a family. Mine didn't and we have lost each other. To this day they have not been willing to try to understand, and I suppose they never will. We have each gone our separate ways. I feel sad, but it is for the best; emotionally we just strangled one another, and they were too keen to blame me for everything, particularly my illness. However, I have now grieved the loss of my family and can express the appropriate sorrow regarding the emotional issues without seeking to name or to blame anyone, nor any one thing.

Blaming someone or something, or finding the reason as to why, somehow always makes us all feel better, even if it is with regard to why we have a cold, or a headache or feel tired. I, too, tend to do this, but regarding eating disorders they are far too complex. There is no one simple reason as to why. It is too easy to look back at our families. We are all a product of our upbringing, (as are our parents, and their parents), and, surely, parents love to the best of their ability at the time, as they know how, but, as is general, maybe that love is not given in the way in which we particularly need it. Not how we need our parents to be in order to make us the person we *think or thought* we can be. Until we forgive them, even though at a certain point we don't condone them, we keep ourselves emotionally a child. We cannot grow up emotionally in a certain aspect of our life and therefore we cannot let that forgiveness come. If we are to do this we have to be ready and willing. Hence, I feel, every family member needs to be ready and willing to work together, where possible, to avoid such issues as blame.

I know too, that it is also impossible to say *why*, as some people would argue. *Why* did I have 'it' – 'it' being anorexia/ bulimia nervosa? Firstly, a person doesn't 'have it', it is not a virus, it is a *chosen* coping mechanism for dealing with emotions (albeit something chosen unwittingly), and secondly there cannot be any one single accountable answer. There are so many hypothetical answers, so many possibilities which people seek, maybe in desperation, maybe for comfort, but there are no real answers. Sure there may be a catalyst that acts as the final straw, and which may have set

164

me off coping in this fashion, but before that, many things were going on. Therefore, the 'cause' if you like, can only be described as the result of a compilation of events, possible traumas and life-experiences. It would be too easy, and very tempting, indeed – but wrong – to tie it all up in one 'nice' easy package; for example, fearing my parents' marriage was failing, and tiring of them arguing, causing me to want to become the centre of attention, which I did by becoming ill. (Resulting in me becoming their joint focal point, and thus keeping them together) Or, upon feeling the weight of what I sensed was my mother's unsatisfied emotional married life, and my father's anger, I turned inwards, into myself, and chose anorexia nervosa as my coping mechanism. Perhaps I never wanted to grow up, perhaps I wanted to be a Peter Pan? perhaps I was tired of being told what to do, and chose something that I could do, to my own standards, without telling anyone, so seeking to lose weight? Perhaps, perhaps, perhaps? Perhaps only this – there may be some truth in some of what I have mentioned, but *no* answers, *no* reasons *why*.

During our lifetimes, we all experience the feelings of being misunderstood, rejected, ridiculed and dismissed. I'm not talking here of great traumatic events. The most painful experiences can arise from surprisingly minor, everyday conversations and events that we may not even recall. They do not stand out, but the response that we get leads us to feel ashamed of these needs, desires and feelings, so we unconsciously lock them away inside. We then develop defences to protect ourselves against anticipated future hurts. My putting my feelings 'on hold' with my eating disorder, was I am sure, my defence, but at the same time my emotional hunger was also a call to be taken more seriously. As a result, food became my weapon, but as I became more and more ill, it also became my enemy and something of which I was terrified. Food, (ie, eating) equalled Fat, and I was scared that food was going to do terrible things to me.

Since leaving my eating disorder behind, Pam, in looking back with me, has described me as being 'intensive and introspective'. I didn't like that description one bit and was eager to contest it, because it hurt, but I can understand its relevance from both sides of the fence, thus agreeing and disagreeing with it at the same time. To the outsider, this may be an obvious and accurate description, but as far as the me inside was concerned, when I was ill, I was not introspective. I was *not* thinking about myself, *my* needs and *my* feelings – I daren't – I was too scared, and was using my anorexia/bulimia as a distraction. 'Insular' was another word which Pam used, but that is something with which I guess I have to entirely agree, bound as I was by my rigid disciplines and routines.

From my own experience, I have to say that I do think the emotions that trigger an eating disorder and eating problems are ultimately knowable. At first, though, they seem completely mysterious and unfathomable, but time and energy devoted to exploring and acknowledging them does help come up with emotional explanations. That time, and energy, however, demands considerable determination and perseverance, and for many reasons. As far as I was concerned, and I am certain this is applicable to everyone, I had to stop trusting my own judgement, and realise that I was *very wrong*. I, therefore, had to place my trust in someone or others, in plural. I had to surrender the need for so much control, and accept that anorexia/bulimia nervosa was solving nothing, only making things worse. Weight was not the issue, rather how I felt and thought underneath all the fear.

Recovery is a very frightening thought because it involves confronting and coping with change and experiencing all kinds of difficult feelings. It is further compounded by the fact that normality does not mean the end of making mistakes, being uncertain, or confused about things and experiencing ups and downs. One has to hang on to the fact that it means being able to cope in a *con*structive and assertive way, not *de*structively.

Of course the other issue is food, and having to eat, as well as learning how to 'eat properly' and be able to stop. As a sufferer you have to remember that food is *not* an enemy. It is only *you* who can do terrible things with food, by using it as a weapon against yourself, and a tool with which to cope with difficult feelings and emotional stress. The natural progression of the illness is the realisation of the trap one falls into in an eating disorder; maintaining the 'buzz' or euphoria means eating less and less if anything is to be achieved, whilst eating more means failure and loss of self-control. I eat now, more, properly and regularly, with a snack or two or whatever, in between my meals and without fear. I realise, now, that being here, ie, being *without* anorexia/bulimia nervosa signifies the success, achievement and self-control I had equated with self-denial only.

It is maybe anger or resentment that keeps the whole illness going, as well as fear of normality and self-deprivation, and it might be quite pertinent at this point to suggest that the secrecy and deceit surrounding eating disorders emphasises what was probably for me, and others, a silent protest against the world. When I was ill, I remember being asked why was I angry, but denied it; one, I was absolutely sure I wasn't angry, and two, if I was, then goodness knows what I was angry about. I felt *hurt* not angry, but during my spell in the clinic, I felt more hurt when I discovered I was indeed angry! It took me a long time to accept and work through the anger, and, also, to acknowledge it as a normal human trait and emotion which we are all allowed to express. I think several of my poems show how angry I was, but this interpretation of them I have only been able to come to since recovering. I spoke of being imprisoned by my eating disorder, and of it being too late and too scary to join the outside world, 'the people you see', but I think I was 'caged' before that, and upon reflection that cage was made up of controls, restraints, disciplines, etc, and other environmental factors that existed around me as a child. My anorexia itself was me angrily rattling the bars of that cage, trying to get out, and perhaps that is a clue with regard helping sufferers to recover. Merely encouraging or forcing them to eat is just trying to stop them rattling the bars, not come out of the cage. Surely with the right therapy, the right help, or counselling to help the person find the key, recovery would be them leaving the cage through the door, opened by this key? They would be leaving behind those afore-mentioned restraints which were operating many years before.

Another pointer to recovery was eliminating my shame, and trying to identify the various rôles that food took on – for example, comforter, suppressor or friend, and exchanging these for real issues and emotions. Help and support, I mistakenly saw as being dependent upon others, ie, losing my own independence, and intrusive, instead of allowing room for sharing, so I had to change that viewpoint and I also had to learn that recovery was not a question of simply stopping; it was a psychological dis-ease with myself, *not* a food fad or 'slimmer's disease' that could be all changed by stopping the behaviour around food.

I know the beginning of my road to recovery was the day Pollyanna surfaced, *with my permission*, after the train suicide attempt. (After all ANN is in PollyANNa!). I finally did the only thing I could do – and had to do, I reckon, – I looked into my void and cried. Cried, because as I looked in, I began to realise there were a lot of things about myself that I didn't like, but which I had to face. As a compulsive people-pleaser, locked into anorexia, I had lived according to the approval of others, and living like that had permitted no change. Likewise, no change of life, job, family, climate or whatever could have possibly helped me. No matter where I went or what I did, the problem was with me. I finally recognised that to have any chance of recovery at all, would mean changing the way I saw myself, saw other people, and how I thought they saw me. I would have to adopt Fritz Perl's 'Gestalt prayer' as my motto: *I am not in this world to live up to [other people's] expectations. And [they] are not in this world to live up to mine.*

Recovery does not mean that I have swept everything under the carpet, nor just stepped into another room. I can still see it all and feel it, but I understand it now and it fails to threaten me. Sweeping under the carpet is a convenient method of avoidance but it does nothing and the dance of death just continues. Avoidance at times seems an easier option, but the battle against an eating disorder is fought in the mind, thus negative feelings do not go away. The only way to avoid using avoidance is to realise how necessary it is to face things, and to have a strong network of support to help, who are not props and who oppose segregation and loneliness. This helps discourage the self disorder, which manifests itself along with the self dis-ease, and perhaps highlights the family's rôle.

So often the sufferer's family and friends blame the sufferer for everything that has, and is, going wrong. This cannot be right. More often than not what has happened, is that the person who is ill has taken upon his/her shoulders the whole weight of the family's problems, as did I. As previously mentioned, blame is dangerous; it will only compound the situation and make the battleground even more formidable. As I worked *with* the medical staff, so the family/friends must work *with* the sufferer. This does not mean pitying him/her, or giving in, for the sake of peace, to whatever he/she does or says, but rather a firm arm of support, that allows room for talking, listening, discussing, and building up trust between each other. Trust is so essential, especially as a person with an eating disorder is a liar. Lying is intrinsic to the disorder; I was no exception. I lied to myself and I lied to others. Lying to myself was the worst, because I kidded myself so well and believed myself. I believed quite wrongly, and dangerously too, that I could stop my behaviour and obsessions any time I wanted to. As a result, I became worse, and more and more ill. In the end I distrusted myself completely, distrusted others, and others began to distrust me. My lying and my silence, (regarding the truth about what was happening), was another use of avoidance. I was avoiding facing my feelings. My anorexia/bulimia created a diversion from all the things with which I could not cope, and I chose to spend my time alone – as a way of avoiding people whom I didn't trust to be able to try and understand. Their pointing out my symptoms, which might be hurting or upsetting them did no good; I wanted to point out back that they didn't understand. So it was better to leave me be, and let me be alone. The relief I felt at the lifting away of all the emotional responsibilities, and people-pressure was far greater than the pain and mental anguish I was suffering, and anyway – initially – I thought it was good – I lost weight.

You don't have to be thin to win. Lean is mean! These days, going to bed for me at night almost gets in the way of living! (So different to those dark years when I used to hide in bed for as much of the day as possible, not wanting to get up, not wanting to acknowledge yet another dawn). I awake early each morning, eager to get on with the day, and having experienced the mental anguish of an eating disorder, find life's problems to be really rather superficial. My motto is that I can do anything and everything I want to do, *providing I really want to do it*. After all, I *really* wanted – eventually – to leave my eating disorder behind, and I did. However, I do know my limitations, too, and as in Rudyard Kipling's poem *If*, I'll not let dreams become my Master, but I will dream – that is a part of living.

Recovery for me was all about meeting challenges head on, taking risks to confront myself and other people, and hanging on to my feelings, to give room for self-analysis and self-examination. It must be the same, I feel, for others. It's not just about *wanting* but *doing*. Not just *wanting* to recover, but being open about the disorder and *doing* something about it, *WITH HELP*. You cannot do it on your own, because you will always tell yourself you can do it tomorrow. But tomorrow never comes.

Recovery is for everyone, but it demands a lot of positive commitment. Being free is not just being free to eat, to be like other 'normal people,' as I thought when I was ill, but to be free to express feelings and emotions – whether they be sadness, fear, anger, happiness, pleasure or whatever – and feel OK. Of course food and meals are a part of it, but it is not the top priority, nor certainly the obsession it is when

170

you are ill. For years I never wanted 'tomorrow', I wanted to be dead, or 'cured', so that I could face it, or so I thought, but tomorrow, when ill, never came; it was always today, so it is *TODAY* that *you* have to take action. Don't consider your eating disorder as an endurance test. If you do that, you are failing already. I can tell you there are many compensations for taking determined steps forward *NOW*, even though the price might seem tremendously terrifying. You see, 'yesterdays' become a hazy memory, the longer you hang on to your eating disorder, 'tomorrows' never come, and 'todays' are so hellish that you begin to not want today either. But it keeps on coming, and just like food, is a normal part of life. Leaving your eating disorder behind is not, therefore, a matter of developing will-power, or control; it signifies an intense ability to respect and accept oneself both physically and mentally, and needs greater in-depth therapy.

I do feel sad and low occasionally, but then doesn't everyone? However, the difference now is that I know the feelings will pass, and I will be laughing again soon. Usually I can trace the trigger – although premenstrually it's a bit hairy! – and once having done that I can acknowledge the feelings and they no longer remain as ominous. I am free to go on – and *ENJOY*. Having never really celebrated good things, I do still find this occasionally difficult to handle. Fun and happiness is sometimes too overwhelming. However, the crying soon stops – and is replaced by laughter and joy. I have a good sense of humour, (so I'm told), and can finally laugh at myself and with others. You see, at last I'm 'one of the crowd', I'm with 'the people (I) see'. I can give and receive. I have finally established a life which allows me to put down roots, and am certainly experiencing the values of friendship – being a friend to others and having friends myself. This does not mean I am being propped up all round in a protective way; I no longer need that. I had a crutch for twenty eight years – my eating disorder – I don't need one any more. Friends, acquaintances and the many new people I meet daily, help to enrich the quality of life, and are people with whom I can share. Sharing – both the good and the bad

– is, for me, anyway, *so* necessary. Some people celebrate or commiserate by going out for the evening or day, possibly incurring considerable expense, but for me it is far simpler. I laugh or cry, as appropriate – and then pick up from where I left off and go on with life, planning, dreaming and doing. I know I'll never regress to the pattern of retracting into my shell. That is history. And my shell was one hell of a solitary cell. I know now there is always a tomorrow, and I want it, but at the same time I want to squeeze out every pennyworth of today.

I would dearly love to prevent people suffering as much as I and my family did, for as long as I did, and from being as I am, now, physically disabled, but I can't. However, one thing I can do is to encourage you all, and tell you all, that there *is* a way out; you can find your key to the door to freedom if you seek help. Don't kid yourself as I did that you can do it and/or will do it on your own. The real truth is you cannot – and you won't, you are your own enemy, and the worst one possible. Step forward, open up and *don't be afraid*. Ask for help by identifying your needs gradually. For certain the agony of examining the underlying issues of your disorder has got to be better than an agonising death and a very sombre funeral. Unfortunately in your illness there is nothing sweet or peaceful about death. It is slow, not quick, so there is barely any relief to be experienced. Peacefully slipping away in sleep may be a myth. You are quite likely to drop dead somewhere.

No-one has had to attend my funeral – although everyone was waiting for it, including me. The cemetery will have to wait. I've overcome the idea of being a failure; I can communicate, be assertive, say no, and laugh at myself. I'm free. I could not, nor can anyone, change the world, nor the pressures or what happened in my life. However I could, and did, eliminate the degree of pressure, and I'm glad I did, because I now realise they were not worth the effort of being so ill. But it took me twenty eight long years, during which time I almost died on several occasions. Recovery isn't about seeking a 'cure', because it is a process that takes a long time.

A process that involves modifying the way in which you think and behave. It demands damn hard work. It's not easy either, it costs a lot of pain, but all I can say is it's worth it. I love living!

You can only make progress by sticking your neck out and taking a risk. Rather like a tortoise, meaning, too, that the progress will be slow. The rapidity with which my eating disorder took over my life, I liken to a ball rolling down a very steep hill. Once it starts it, (I), went down very fast indeed. Coming back up is, unfortunately, a really hard task, but if you have all that energy to channel into your eating disorder and keep up with its fast downhill pace, then somewhere inside you, you have the energy to turn it round, and face the uphill challenge of recovery. I'm nobody special in having done this, and if you think I am, turn that thought into a question, and ask yourself what's so special about *you* that you cannot recover too? For a long time, unable to die, I began to resign myself to my eating disorder. This, it seemed, was how I was going to be for the rest of my life. I was one of those people who, when their boat comes in, is at the airport! In realising that I need not accept this as my lot, though, I'm back up the hill, and I certainly haven't got back up here to go downhill again. I'm free to get on with living – and the next meal – and have a chocolate or two, if I want one! I no longer have to act on my feelings and eat several packets of biscuits or cereal in one go, or starve for a week. I believe in myself, I trust myself, and at long last, I can be true to myself. I feel wonderful! I love laughing and life continues to be a fascinating journey of discovery, with capital 'F's for its Fascination and Fun!

As a sufferer, the horrible realisation you have to acknowledge is that you can only get worse, not better, unless *you* do something to try and stop it. There is no such thing as getting to, or maintaining an ideal size, you are kidding yourself if you think there is. An obsession like an eating disorder, demands perfection, demands more all the time, and you never win. You do not have to reach the pits and depths of despair as did I in order to talk or need help.

Try and arrest it now. Life is not worth postponing until the day slimness comes, because if you are anorexic, you will never be thin enough, and as a bulimic your wish, when asked what you want out of life, being to have all the cakes you can eat without getting fat, is impossible, because you can never have enough of what you don't really want. You cannot starve or stuff your feelings away. Life can be engaged in with whatever size you are, and, albeit this meaning taking risks, and meeting challenges head on, which hurt a lot, on that bumpy road to recovery, whilst you try to unearth the underlying issues of your disorder, you *can* do it. *I* know you can do it. I *believe* you can do it. You, too, must try and adopt this positive attitude, because once you feel positive, you will be able to look inside yourself, and start the necessary self-examination and self-analysis – known professionally as cognitive thinking. Why don't you join me now dancing for joy, instead of dancing on your grave? Why don't you, too, taste ice cream, chips, honey or beans on toast? And why not start today – so that, like me, you know who 'me' is, and become proud of 'me', and then maybe identify earnestly and honestly with a poem I wrote in my logbook on 23rd January 1991:

I want my shape – I don't want to be thin.
I like my shape – it's feminine.
– it's ME – and at long last I like ME,
Yes! Ann is OK. People seem to like her,
And I do, too!
I've stopped dancing on my grave.
The cemetery is not for me.
I was never meant to die,
– dying as I tried – to be thin.
But thinness was not really my goal.
Perhaps I wanted to be a child, as opposed to a
    woman?
Because adults liked me.
They liked to protect me, and care for me,
And I felt wanted – but never needed,

174

Until men came, who liked fucking children
– or rather women with childish bodies.
It gave power to their ego, but deflated mine,
And I didn't want any responsibilities.
I couldn't see myself as a woman
– with a figure, with curves, firm and shapely.
This wasn't me.
And I couldn't accept myself as a woman.
I wanted so much – emotionally.
I needed, and wanted to be needed.
Lack of shape, and deprivation became my escape
*   route,*
I turned inwards, and left the table.
But now I'm back! – as a woman, and still with
*   needs,*
But I have goals, aims, and dreams, now,
Because my 'danse macabre' is over, and I now
*   dance for joy.*

The voluntary work that I have chosen to do today – my telephone help-line, initiating two self-help groups, my writings and co-counselling – I do because I want to turn my years of illness into a constructive experience from which sufferers, and non-sufferers, alike, may understand more, and more importantly, realise the necessity to try to learn and understand more. Eating disorders are not silly fads; they are (potentially, anyway) serious killers. Society's attitudes are so pitiful, sad and downright ignorant! It is so easy to believe that someone is all right when they look OK or better, a problem akin to both the anorectic – 'eating properly' and 'putting on weight' – and the bulimic, who appears to be a normal weight. Few people realise that the disorder, a problem in itself, incurs further problems in the recovery process; discovering normality is new, hard, and sometimes terrifying. The physical recovery requires therapy in order to heal the mind, as well, and straighten out the thinking.

I feel the lack of understanding surrounding eating disorders is becoming worse, and sufferers are the butt end of

175

many a joke, for example 'the typical middle-class family, you know, the one with the anorexic daughter', (Victoria Wood 'As seen on TV' series). There is too much alignment too, I think, to dieting, because there is a great difference between the serious dieter and the person with an eating disorder. Society appears to see only the similarities. Maybe they are too scared to notice anything else, but then in all fairness to society, if eating disorders are so secretive, why should they indeed see any further? Hence, perhaps, the jokes. Certainly both dieting and eating disorders are obsessional about calories and 'keeping to the rule', and the whole day could be upset by what the weighing scales say in the morning, which dictates the wardrobe for the day. (Baggy clothing if you feel lousy, or fat, figure-hugging clothing if you feel good, or thin). It seems that regarding the subject of dieting, society encourages us not to like each other; everyone wants to be envied, and everyone wants to have the ideal figure. Weighing scales, tape-measures, weighing charts, fridge-stickers, and low-calorie foods dictate styles of living. However, many diets don't work, a testimony, perhaps to the fact that one cannot live by sheer will-power alone, and this is perhaps the major difference between the dieter and the anorectic. As does the dieter rely on will-power to cut out and down on food so the anorectic thinks he/she is. But, the dieter is usually over-weight in the first place and sets a target weight, whilst the anorectic has no stopping point, no goal, just thinness, which is never achieved, because he/she is never thin enough, and cannot define the word 'thin'. Further, there is a good possibility that he or she was not overweight beforehand, either. As far as I was concerned, the distortion of self-body image can be paralleled to the distorted view of myself as a person, and my view, too, of how everyone else saw me. I was never good/nice/helpful/ sociable/whatever enough, therefore I couldn't bear my legs touching at the top, let alone hear the sound of my jeans or tights rubbing together as I walked. They were too fat. I had certain ways of sitting, too, so that my thighs didn't splay out. Rather there was a gap between them – that cats and babies would often fall through if they sat on my lap – if I could sit thin then that was good. I loved it. The thinner I got, the greater the possibility of being thought of in a good light by others, was the way my mind thought.

I consider dieting to be too much of a social hobby and pressure, and a dangerous one. Not that I feel this is the trigger of an eating disorder at all, but it is something which provides and encourages a medium for self-punishment, for example, 'I won't go out with my friends tonight, perhaps I'll go in a few days time, when I'm lighter.' It affects relation-ships because we are trained to judge through the outer body, and appearances, as opposed to who we are, and what we can actually do. The equation seems to be, 'I'm fat – I'm miserable, I'm useless. When I'm thinner, I'll be happy'. This sort of attitude is very close to touching on the anorectic atti-tude, and food is becoming the tool with which a mother may threaten her crying child – 'No tea unless you start behaving'. It is all too useful in this respect, and almost everybody uses it in the reward or punishment system, to some degree. However, for those without an eating *disorder* it is a temporary thing; for those *with* an eating disorder it is a sinister manifestation of much that is wrong, and is causing dis-ease.

Recovery for me has meant I am now able to be assertive instead of passive, and I have learnt to distinguish between physiological hunger and emotional hunger, so am therefore able to respond to each appropriately, as well as identify my needs. In working with the help-line, the groups, and coun-selling, I have also learned a lot, and gained much, too. Sadly, though, in these few years during which I have received much publicity and made my own little contribu-tions, I feel the only progress that has been made is that 'anorexia nervosa' and 'bulimia nervosa' have become very topical issues. They still remain dirty words and there is very little talk about compulsive eating and overeating, and anything we do hear of, is still linked to a 'slimmer's disease'. They may be recognised words now, but still very few people understand, or appreciate, their meaning. It is still very difficult, and sometimes impossible for sufferers to admit to their problem; many hide it from husbands or wives, boyfriends or girlfriends, friends and family. Even though they may have been ill for as long as eight years or more, they have still managed to keep it a secret. And it is a dreadful, deadly secret, of which no-one knows; the problem, behavioural patterns and routines are so well disguised and hidden.

The non-sufferer needs to realise that they *can* help, but there is no set time or period in which recovery is reached. It is a long, slow process, that demands hanging on together, holding one another's hand tight, and being honest about how you all feel. If the sufferer is making you tire, or you feel it is time you had some space, then tell him or her. Over-protectiveness and trying to wrap him or her in cotton wool is really ignoring the problem. Use of avoidance, again. It is also saying 'Don't worry we love you as you are', when you should be saying 'Don't worry, we love you, but we don't like your anorexia/bulimia/whatever, and if we are to remain together we must be honest with one another'. There will be many a slip back, but that should not be seen by either party as a failure. It is normal. After all, think of the prisoner who is released from prison after serving a long jail sentence. The outside world is unfamiliar, and he may feel so insecure that he re-offends in order to return to the only life he now knows, frightened of establishing something new.

Another issue that also occurs is in the tirelessly asked question, 'What is the point?' I remember asking Pam that very question, one day in Bournemouth, after returning from a weighing session and discovering I had lost one pound, which I had to regain. In tears, I asked her what was the point? Why was I doing this? Who for? There was nobody to do it for, and, anyway, why bother? Was life and living only about making sure I kept to the correct weight now? She answered in the most poignant of ways. It is something I vividly recall, and will always remember. She likened the road to recovery, and the journey of discovery, to a bus journey, perhaps a mystery tour. You know when you start, and when the bus stops you can get off, as and if you want

178

to, but, as Pam said, 'If you don't go all the way, you'll never know the answer to your question.' How true!

So, I decided upon the whole of the bus-ride, and was at the harbour when the boat came in – and I thoroughly recommend it! Just to be is wonderful. There doesn't *have* to be a reason for everything, and being positive all the time isn't always possible. I find it especially difficult when my pain threshold is low, and I have to spend a few days resting in bed, unable, sometimes to switch off that pain button. I try to continue my 'work' from bed, but my eating disorder has also left another legacy. I tire quite easily, so sometimes I have to give in and stay on one level of the house for the day. (We have adapted our bedroom and bathroom, so that I can cook for us both up there, continue with my hobbies, answer the help-line or whatever). It is still worth it, though. Life is so qualitative – I love living, and enjoy so much, and have such fun, even if it's a matter of having to play the 'glad game' at times. And this is for everyone. As Pooh said to Christopher Robin, after Christopher Robin asked him what he liked doing best in the world: 'What I like best in the whole world is ME and Piglet going to see You, and You saying "What about a little something?" and Me saying, "Well, I shouldn't mind a little something, should you, Piglet," and it being a hummy sort of day outside, and birds singing.'

Perhaps you would like to remember this, because as a sufferer although your greatest wish is to be better, but still thin, the reality is you cannot be both, and the truth, when you recover, is that you will be quite content with 'a little something' and enjoying a 'hummy sort of day' without any self-imposed pressures or routines. Like me.

179

'HELP!' AND HELP

The cry of 'help' and the response to help are very difficult areas within eating disorders. Invariably the sufferer crying for help doesn't know exactly what he or she wants, beyond being able to be normal around food, and yet still remain thin, and the person responding to the call invariably doesn't know what to do. Quite often the sufferer is being put under pressure to recover by others. It becomes necessary at this point for the sufferer to be able to identify his or her own emotional needs, and go beyond the frustrations and the disillusionment of *feeling* and not *being* fat. No-one can appreciate themselves whilst hating their body. I finally saw that after twenty years of dancing on my grave, dying, literally, to be thin. I needed to work from the inside out, from my emotions, my feelings, and, perhaps, my dreams, rather than from the outside in approach, which began with my outer appearance, my body. And, I feel this is, generally speaking, the only way to a full recovery, although I do appreciate – from speaking to various medics, and to the callers on my help-line – that starting with the outside in approach is more appropriate sometimes.

The identity crises through which I sometimes go with regard to my weight do, sometimes, seem all quite unfathomable, incomprehensible and daft. Quite stupid, too. For example, I may weigh in at eight stones one pound and feel enormous, or my weight may read eight stones three pounds yet I feel thin! Possibly this is one part of the reason that makes eating disorders the serious killer they are – because at times it does seem complete double-dutch and nothing

180

more. I can feel 'fat-fat' ie, lumpy, splodgy and wobbly, for example, or 'fat-slim' ie, heavy, or 'slim-fat', ie, OK, but a bit more heavy than I would like the scales to say! I think, though, that this more than ever highlights the psychological aspect of weight, and shows the emotional link attached to size. The issue of weight disguising the emotions.

When I was ill I felt utterly alone, in a crazy self-destructive world. When I entered the clinic, scared as I was of meeting other people with a similar disorder, the value of finding that someone else could share and/or identify with my hell was almost magical, and such a relief. Not merely to talk about the symptoms – the negative feelings and the extreme behavioural patterns and depths of despair, to which you sink – but also to speak more graphically and with integrity, about feelings and events.

I am certain that most sufferers from an eating disorder need to be filled up. Filled up *EMOTIONALLY*, not necessarily physically; this whether they be purging and/or eating to excess, or whether they are starving, or eating a little and then vomiting. The help they need is hope and belief that they *can* recover. Understanding, too, that their freedom doesn't simply signify stepping out of a prison cell into another room, but rather into a wide open space – with no barriers or limitations – something that can continue forever, and is endless. The recovery process is founded on an holistic approach therefore providing succour for both body and mind. Sufferers need to consider themselves and seek help to help themselves, as whole beings.

I, unfortunately, went to the extremes of having to be hospitalised on many occasions, to eventually acknowledge my disorder and to decide whether or not to commit myself to recovering. No-one need be as ill as I was, or indeed, as *lucky* as I was, to get a place in a hospital in time – ie, before they die, but they must be willing to seek help for themselves and take action themselves. If you don't step forward yourself, I can assure you, no-one will step forwards to you. It is indeed, quite true that laugh and the world laughs with you, but cry and you cry alone. As I have said before, the bigger the support team there is to help you in the recovery process, the better, and one method of self-help – which avoids the (sometimes) fearsome world of psychiatry and medics – is group therapy, by way of self-help groups.

I remember thinking at one time when I was ill, that I couldn't possibly go to an eating disorder group, because I might meet other anorectics who were thinner than me, as well as possibly meeting somebody I knew. I was frightened that I wouldn't be thin enough, and that we might get into competition to see who could become the thinnest, who had the worst symptoms, etc. If that is what *you* think, then I suggest you seriously ask yourself whether you are really motivated to try to recover, and realise that, if you are not, then you are saying the equivalent of 'Let me be. I want to keep my anorexia/bulimia/whatever'. I would, though, also suggest that envy and competitive feelings are more an expression of your internal feelings about not accepting yourself, and being convinced that you have no right to life and the good things it has to offer. The competitive feelings are almost a psychological stick with which to beat yourself, to reinforce your underlying feelings of exclusion and inadequacy. They were for me; and I see, now, the importance of those two emotions – envy or jealousy, and competitiveness, as feelings that need to be acknowledged and expressed. They are a quite normal human trait, but within the parameters of anorexia and bulimia they can be a deadly weapon.

Within a self-help structure the group members are able to decide what they want to say, and how much, and how they want to be helped. This I think, helps them to develop confidence and trust in themselves and in other people. Trust is a key issue, because intrinsic to an eating disorder is much deceit and dishonesty, even if it is just *self*-deceit and *self*-dishonesty. You will get feedback from others, and give feedback to them, so it becomes a sort of co-counselling. Often what you will confront in these times will be difficult, painful, confusing and sometimes incomprehensible and too distressing. However, there is the support of fellow sufferers

182

around you, and a group leader, perhaps counsellor, to give objective opinions and/or advice or guidance if needs be.

You will need to be prepared to listen to yourself, with the same caring attention you give to others. So often it becomes easier to negate your own feelings and problems by concentrating on those of others. You must not let other peoples' problems minimise your own; if they are a problem to you, then they are a problem full stop! Everyone is unique, everyone is special, and the combination of each person's uniqueness shapes a group and gives it its' particular flavour. So the group is essentially what the group makes it.

Because you are embarking upon an experiment to help you focus on aspects of what makes you tick, you will be using the group to explore your individuality. What makes you 'you', and the kinds of experiences that have led you to eat or not to eat and to behave as you do, meaning you use your body, weight, shape, size and food to express yourself. Anger, tension, envy, sadness, tears and distrust will all surface. But laughter too. You may try to focus on other peoples' problems, taking on the role of listener. You may take an active or passive role, positive or assertive. It doesn't really matter what 'type' or 'category' you fall into, and as long as you remember you are there *FOR YOURSELF* the provision of a safe, trusting environment is what it's all about. You therefore have as much right to talk as anyone else, and cry, or express yourself in any way you wish for that matter; focusing on yourself is why you are there. Self-centred though it may feel, remember self-centeredness is necessary, to a degree because it permits self-examination and inner reflection, along with discoveries about other relationships. Things inside and outside, cannot be bad if and when talked about they lead to a more qualitative life for you, and a future.

Don't worry about talking; getting started can be difficult, I know. It may be extra difficult for you because you feel reluctant to believe anything can change. So you've got to think Positive, because change things certainly can. I'm proof! I'm sure, and it seems true, that a group will only work if you each put something into it, and are prepared to work hard. The tremendous temptation to believe or hope that once you are in such a group, your problems just disappear, is bullshit! I cannot emphasise enough that this will not happen. Only by active observation, listening, and intervention will your eating, and body concepts, shift. You might be able to offer each other suggestions, and ask questions, and people might help you when it comes to saying how fat or thin you look. I'm described as slim, sometimes thin, but may feel fat, or my legs feel huge, but I have now learnt that an emotion has probably triggered that feeling, and so am usually able to quickly identify it. And the fatness, hugeness, usually subsides.

If you decide to attend, or even help to set up a self-help group, or indeed decide to set up one yourself, you must make it a *commitment*. Give yourself a trial period of at least three months making the day and time of your meeting sacrosanct. Don't just try it out once and then stop. That's a bit like trying to get into the sea on a nice day; you stick your big toe in, and that's it! It feels too cold to go in any further, so you go back to the beach. However, when you do get into the water, once there, it is OK and you usually enjoy the swim. I cannot promise you self-help meetings will be enjoyable, exactly, but I hope you can appreciate the analogy. Try and remember it, because I don't think you *will* like it at first, or worse still you may like it to begin with, but find it too intimidating a little later on, making you feel very vulnerable, as the group gets to know you better. There will, I'm sorry to say, be a lot of pain around, but, hopefully, some gain, too! So, make the group a weekly, or whatever, priority. Allow yourself time and space to bring up your fears, despairs, frustrations, worries and advances in the group. Learn from your own experiences, and from each other. Patient therapy can only be invaluable if you are all motivated, because then there is mutual support for one another. The atmosphere generated, will be one of tremendous concern, purpose, trust and confidentiality.

There is one other very important thing to remember in all this, and that is that by going to a self-help group, you are not alienating yourself from your family or friends, or from professional help. That attitude could be unconstructive, and indeed, characterises part of the problem underlying eating disorders. Rather it should be seen as meaning that the person with the disorder is committed to changing to a better kind of self-regulation, (and to shrugging off the disorder, if at all possible), meaning the non-sufferer should view it as a positive move that needs support and encouragement. The group may be one that allows a close friend or family to attend, too, but as to whether that be a good or a bad idea is a very personal choice.

Beating an eating disorder is a complicated process. There are very few specialist services for sufferers, and it isn't only the specialists who can help; in fact, I would very definitely say that it is a case where specialists cannot always help. Something I'm sure with which even they would agree. Whatever help is available, anyway, is not a magic cure or formula, it is all about helping you to help yourself. No-one holds the magic wand or key. Only you can do it in the end, and you have to want to do it in the beginning – and the beginning, remember is *today*. Tomorrow never comes! This is not to say as I have mentioned that the whole responsibility of trying to recover rests on your shoulders alone. Taking that attitude once again eptimises the essence of eating disorders, – the wish/need/no-alternative-but attitude to be alone. You need, and this is a must, to recognise the problem in a broader context than eating behaviour, and that it is, for you, a major problem, that warrants help rather than scorn, or dismissal, from others. Or from yourself, for that matter. An eating disorder is very costly; it is a full-time job, and as the condition progresses, the costs become more evident. People who do choose to remain in contact with you may do so in response to you as an invalid; it is not because they are 'understanding'. Likewise GPs who are also described in the same context. I disagree – they are merely 'tolerant'. Meanwhile, life leaves you behind, and unless you take action immediately, I can tell you this realisation happens many years after the onset of the problem, leaving an awful feeling that it is too late to catch up. Having once *chosen* to be alone, I found myself *having* to be alone, and was, therefore, very lonely. In the beginning 'let me be' was my choice, but in the end there was no choice. I *had* to be alone, I had pushed everyone away.

In choosing to escape from the grip of your eating disorder, you have two choices: escape by recovering completely, or be a better adapted anorectic/bulimic/compulsive/overeater. I have spoken above of self-help groups, but if you cannot face them, or indeed there are not such resources near you, you can still help yourself, and it is here that I would again refer to my logbook and diaries. However, one thing I would say is don't rush into attempts to recover, unless you have considered the full implications, and you have the necessary resources around you. Trying to 'eat properly' and, therefore, in the case of the anorectic, in particular, gain weight, or at least stop losing weight, can become and inevitably does become, extremely terrifying. Putting the food issue aside or 'on hold' whilst you try and understand what on earth you are doing and why, on the other hand, is futile, and merely an excuse for you to continue living within your eating disorder. (Not 'eating properly', or re-learning about eating, means you are still not in touch with the inner you – your thoughts, ideas, opinions, and feelings, – you are still starving, stuffing, bingeing, purging, or vomiting them away). Both issues have to be looked at together, and the inside you is best recorded in writing – although I didn't think so when I first entered the clinic. Across the front of my logbook, I wrote:

'I'm never going to use this thing! I cannot write anything because everything is too important and impossible to put into words'.

The value of using my logbook and diary, in which to record my emotions, was that I realised if I kept putting the emphasis on food or weight, I was just going to go round and round in circles. I began to realise that food and weight were only important because they were the thoughts and feelings with which I was totally pre-occupied. My objective had to be to recognise new emotions, so that I could perhaps realise my temptation to skip some food, or my feelings of being fat, were linked into a concern about something else, – for example, a financial situation. After a considerable period, I began to develop more insight into the 'inside me', and as time went by, and I looked back on my writings, I was able to see how I had changed. I still look back to my logbook occasionally today. It is interesting, and very helpful to see familiar patterns developing, and it is also very encouraging. It confirms that I *am* now fully recovered, and that, yes, I *did* suffer a chronic eating disorder! (I often wonder, these days, as I enjoy some passion cake and coffee mid-afternoon, without thought of calories, weight-gain, etc, did I really have an eating disorder? It sometimes seems just like a horrible nightmare).

Obviously, what you write is private, but I found showing it to (selected) people to be very valuable, even though it was intensely personal. In doing so, not only was I able to gain their perspective on my thoughts, but I was able to try to *help them*. Help them understand how I felt, and, how, in the later stages, when I reached my target weight, that appearing *physically* better is not the same as *being* better. I have also found my logbook to be very important in my marriage. Steve elected to read quite a bit, and it has helped him comprehend a little more about some of the emotional scars which sometimes show through. It was his choice, just as it was his suggestion that *we* take over the responsibility of the weigh-ins. Instead of me visiting the doctor twice weekly, we, together, visit our local chemist, and record my weight on a visual chart – an important thing to do in order to see just how well or otherwise I am maintaining. We now weigh in monthly, though, after rigidly adhering to weekly sessions for eighteen months after I moved to Hastings. By then I was beginning to feel that the weighing scales were becoming my crutch for maintaining my weight, rather than me using my own judgement over food quantities, etc, as well as learning to respond to physical hunger in an appropriate way, and be more adventurous with the great variety of foods around!

Slipping back, and hiccups along the way, are a natural part of the recovery process, and should not be seen as failure. However, if constant attendance with a therapist, counsellor or psychiatrist, regular self-help group attendance, and/or writing, becomes merely habit – maybe a 'time-filler' – then repeated hiccups may indeed mean failure, because it brings up the possibility that there is a part of you that does not want to let go your eating disorder. I found that a very hard thing to acknowledge, although I recognised it was true. So, in identifying that my particular need, then, was for help to work out why part of me didn't want to let go anorexia, I was, in fact, able to progress.

It is very hard to let go of life with an eating disorder, because you have to give up one identity, (the only one I felt I knew), without having yet found another one, and it feels very unsafe. For a long while I felt a 'nobody'; anorexia/bulimia nervosa was the only life I knew, and often I tortured myself with thoughts that I might have 'jumped out of the frying pan into the fire'! However, in time, I realised that the 'frying pan' was a fire, too, and I had jumped into something *far better* and was beginning to be able to laugh, for example, at all the 'foody' expressions I was using, in my writings in order to recognise my feelings. Such phrases included 'having my cake and eating it', 'the icing on top of the cake', 'going the whole hog', 'out of the frying pan into the fire', 'fish-face', 'eating humble pie', 'toffee-nosed cow'(!), 'egg-head', 'food for thought', 'sick to death', 'fed up to the back teeth', 'taking the biscuit', and other such idioms! One has to laugh! I did – and it has often made me think, with these various expression abounding, and our current attitudes to food, is it any wonder that eating problems, disorders, abuse, are so integral a part of our lifestyle?

I have mentioned the *self*-help stage first, for several reasons, perhaps the main two being that firstly, by the time one joins the queues, and/or receives professional help, the deterioration is much increased, and, secondly, professional

188

help for me, in the first instance, anyway, appeared to make things a great deal worse. Admittedly, I had no contact with eating disorder specialists, but to discover that the professionals did not 'understand' either, was alarming, and most of the time, the counselling useless. I was very critical, then, too, – I did not seem to like, get on with, or relate to, anyone, nor them to me, and, although I very much accept the importance of finding a therapist with whom you *do* feel you can build up trust, (and that there are such issues as personality clashes), I do wonder if inside of all of us – ie, those suffering an eating disorder – is obstinate resistance. This comprising either the firm belief that no-one *can* help, (ie, *their* shortcomings), or no-one *will* be allowed to help, (ie, *us* putting the barriers up), because the help on offer is rarely, if ever, directive. Advice, guidance, 'the answer', was the help *I* wanted, and in longing for this, I found the professional services very frustrating. In fact, I think it may be a correct observation to say that *most* therapy appeared to be scrupulously non-directive, which, for me then, was very alarming. Now, though, having gone through that form of therapy, with specialist help, all I can say is that as long as you remember that recovery from an eating disorder means hanging on to your feelings in order that you can express them constructively, and identify your needs *yourself*, then it is to your favour. Therapy warrants *you* identifying the help you need, (even if it means an hour's session in silence, whilst you try!) and *you doing* and *showing* the motivation, with support, so that you can take on some of the responsibility for your recovery, and relearn, and regain the ability to find yourself, by recognising your feelings.

It seems, I know, that this business of recovery is unfairly demanding. There is a lot you, the sufferer, is required to do. Perhaps the best way of looking at it is as I did – 'I got there (so ill) so I've got to get out (recover) – to hell with everything else.' Further, as with everything, recovery, too has costs, as well as benefits, and I feel it would be very unfair of me to let slip any that I can share.

189

Clearly – and more so as far as the non-sufferer is concerned, perhaps – recovery is ultimately only for the good, but there is one possible cost that often goes hidden, making I'm afraid, recovery even more demanding and more difficult. The loss of family and/or some friends. Choice to and help to recover, may incur a serious loss like this as it did me, and is maybe something of which you should all be aware. I don't think for one moment that it in any way outweighs the benefits of recovery, but it can be a very sad time, for which one is better off if warned. It could possibly hinder recovery, too, if you are not prepared.

As I have already mentioned, recovery involves change, which the family and/or friends must also acknowledge because as you recover, and change, so they will have to, if your relationship is to continue. So often this is not fully realised or understood. Indeed it was not by my parents, nor by some of my friends. Many families to whom I now talk, seem to think the sooner their daughter, son, wife or husband 'gets better', the better will be the relationship between them, and better too, the family relationships. But quite often this is not so. It may be because the only mutual focal point holding a marriage together is the sibling's illness. It may be because the changed relationship, now with someone more assertive, and not ill, is something with which they cannot cope. It may, for the spouse or friend of a recovered anorectic, be because it shows up the anorexia as having been intrinsic to the relationship. Between the two of you, and the two aforesaid family relationships, the roles were clearly nurse and invalid. Now both have to change, and both are equal. This is often very difficult to adjust to, and very intimidating too, sometimes for the ex-nurse. Consequently, there is sadly much separation of families and divorce within marriages. Friends may just drop away.

As I saw this in my own life-experience, I was at first devastated, and then very sad and angry. However, I try to be pragmatic. It had to be if I was to recover. I don't consider it anyone's fault, least of all mine. The point of recovery signified time to move on, to move forward to new

190

things, and put the rest behind me, if I was going to enjoy living. It also demanded acceptance of the situation. So, if this is a choice you maybe have to consider, beware the cost. Perhaps all I should say is good luck.

As I answer all my help-line calls, – from both here and abroad, occasionally – I am very saddened by the stark fact that help for eating disorder sufferers is very, very limited indeed, whether it be professional, as an in-patient, or out-patient, or by way of telephone help-lines, and self-help groups. Is this due to ignorance, I wonder. I think so but is 'ignorance *really* bliss'? Certainly, non-sufferers not involved in any way with an eating disorder, might consider this to be so, but those who *are* involved, find the ignorance frustrating, and often frightening.

So often I am asked by mothers, fathers, husbands, wives, boyfriends, girlfriends, relatives, and friends, how they can help and am bound to reply that they do have a vital role to play, although at the same time, they may sense they are being made to feel intrusive. When you are living with the chaos, distress or despair that an eating disorder can provoke, and the secretiveness, which serves to arouse your suspicions that something may be going on, your feelings of not knowing what to do, make it very difficult indeed to concentrate on more than surviving from day to day, being careful about what you say, and how you say it. There is also the problem of how you are going to deal with each mealtime. Involvement with a sufferer should not mean dictating their lifestyle, but offering a supportive atmosphere which recognises that the sufferer, and you have to be willing to go beyond the symptoms of food, body, weight, and shape, to look at emotions. The starting point, for which, must involve helping the sufferer to reconstruct what was happening in their lives *before* eating problems began, as well as *when* the eating problems began. This will not provide the answer, the reason, as to 'why', but at the same time it is not irrelevant or indulgent. Certainly it may be *distressing*, and that may appear to make the situation worse, but if you and the sufferer start to experience the same distress, an emotion such as sadness, or fear, you possibly have a starting point. My strongest emotion, initially, was fear. Within my eating disorder, I could only channel it into fears of food, and fears of being fat, but once I got beyond that point and started relating that emotion to the meaning of my shape, my sense of self – sexually and socially – family relationships, etc, in my logbook, I found the 'inside' fears, and, slowly, started looking beyond – past the symptoms.

During the latter period of my illness – when I just could not die – and during my stay in the clinic, I always vowed that, if I ever 'got through this', then I would help others. An easy thing to say, but quite a hard thing to do, although I enjoy what I do. However, one often hears this sort of remark following a big operation and a long stay in hospital, for example. The patient has experienced so much kindness and encouragement from the nursing staff, that the relief of recovery makes them feel that when totally fit, they would like to repay the hospital in kind. It is my reckoning, though – and I am now considering both eating disorders and general illnesses – that quite often the opposite happens. Once the recuperation period is over, the patient wants to put the memories and the trauma behind them, and get on with their (new) life. This, of course, is very understandable, and not to be condemned. Certainly, at times, during my work, I do re-experience some of the pain, but it is not enough to drag me down emotionally. My only fear is what will happen the day I step down, which may be because I don't feel able to help any more – already the memories of 'being there' are fading. Or perhaps I may feel too overloaded, because of the demand on my time. Or, on the other hand it might be there comes a time when, quite simply, I, too, want to put it all behind me. The fear is that when I step down, no-one will step up. The problem of eating disorders is a great one, now, and it is on the increase, rapidly. No doubt, it will be worse when, I feel, in maybe two, ten, or even twenty years time, it is right to step into the background. I know that I am strong enough to not let that cloud my judgement, as regards doing what *I* want, but it will not

192

prevent me feeling very sad, so already I am trying to think of other avenues for setting up networks throughout the country, so that no-one need feel alone. One such thought emerged from one of the self-help groups. The suggestion was that names (perhaps) and/or addresses/telephone numbers, be left with receptionists at doctors' surgeries, requesting contact with someone with anorexia, bulimia, compulsive or over eating. This, of course, warrants a very brave step forward by sufferers, and perhaps the surgeries could welcome, and encourage the motivation. 'We are not asking them to do anything', as one lady said, 'only help us to do something ourselves.' No doubt doctors receptionists would be most alarmed at this suggestion. However, maybe it is the seed of a much greater idea begging further thought and consideration and compromise all round.

I welcome any suggestions, and praise any attempts by others to initiate help in order to respond to the (so many) cries of 'help'. And I encourage you to, and to help, too, yourself. Picture someone in the dead of night, eating all the left-overs from restaurant rubbish bags and public dustbins, vomiting and shitting as she goes, and, maybe, in the mad frenzy, actually bingeing on some of that vomit or shit. Disgusting? Yes, but *desperate* – I did it; I also, in various hospital admissions, binged out of the slops. There are many others doing it too, so please think about that word 'HELP', whether you are asking for it, or giving it, because the right help, identified, and the right help given, goes towards producing another 'h' – Happiness, and if it's not happiness that is the ultimate goal in trying to shrug off an eating disorder, then it is (good) Health which encompasses a well being with a well mind.